Hg2|Istanbul

Çırağan Palace

A Hedonist's guide to…

Istanbul

Written by Kathryn Tomasetti
& Tristan Rutherford

A Hedonist's guide to Istanbul

Written by Kathryn Tomasetti & Tristan Rutherford

PUBLISHER – Tremayne Carew Pole
EDITING – Nick Clarke
DESIGN – Nick Randall
MARKETING – Marilyn MacDonald
MAPS – Richard Hale & Nick Randall
REPRO – Advantage Digital Print
PUBLISHER – Filmer Ltd

First edition written and photographed by Nick Hackworth

Email – info@hg2.com
Website – www.hg2.com
Published in the United Kingdom in 2012 by
Filmer Ltd
10th Floor, Newcombe House,
45 Notting Hill Gate, London W11 3LQ

ISBN – 978-1-905428-42-7

This book is dedicated to Antonia Spanos Shanks for opening our eyes to another side of this magical city.

In London we're eternally grateful to James Wolseley Shanks, Constantine Azar, Mehmet Bey, Michael Furniss, William and Myles Howorth, Isabella and Ted Tomasetti, Jill Guest from London's Turkish Culture & Tourism Office, and Sophie Black and Nicole Samson at PRco,

In Istanbul, thanks to Piotr Zalewski, Jonathan Lewis, Kim Tuong, Simon Allen, Martin Selsøe Sørensen, Constanze Letsch, Claudia Wiens, Jennifer Hattam, John 'Polymath' Crofoot, Selim Özcan, Celal Biyiklioğlu at TomTom, Tia Graham at WHotel, Esin Sungur at the Pera Palace, Zeynep Akan and Ceylan Yuceoral at SALT, Sibel Benli at the Four Seasons, Sedat Nemli and Pelin Ulusoy at Edition. In Ankara thanks also to Samuel Roy, Helena Storm, Stratos Efthymiou and Bengi Lostar at the Turkish Ministry of Culture.

Hg2 | Istanbul

How to…

A Hedonist's guide to Istanbul is broken down into easy-to-use sections: Sleep, Eat, Drink, Snack, Party, Culture, Shop, Play and Info. In each section you'll find detailed reviews and photographs. At the front of the book is an introduction to Istanbul and an overview map, followed by introductions to the main areas and more detailed maps. On each of these maps, the places we have featured are laid out by section, highlighted on the map with a symbol and a number. To find out about a particular place simply turn to the relevant section, where all entries are listed alphabetically. Alternatively, browse through a specific section (e.g. Eat) until you find a restaurant you like the look of. Surrounding your choice will be a coloured box – each colour refers to a particular area of the Istanbul. Simply turn to the relevant map to find the location.

Book your hotel on Hg2.com

We believe that the key to a great Istanbul break is choosing the right hotel. Our unique site now enables you to browse through our selection of hotels, using the interactive maps to give you a good feel for the area as well as the nearby restaurants, bars, sights, etc., before you book. Hg2 has formed partnerships with the hotels featured in our guide to bring them to readers at the lowest possible price. Our site now incorporates special offers from selected hotels, as well information on new openings.

The concept

Ever had the feeling, when in an exciting new city, that its excitements were eluding you? That its promise failed to be delivered because you lacked the keys to unlock it? That was exactly what happened to Hg2's founder, Tremayne Carew Pole, who, despite landing in Budapest equipped with all the big-name travel guides, ended up in a turgidly solemn restaurant when all he wanted was a cool locals' hangout. After a wasted weekend, he quit his job and moved to Prague to write the first Hg2 guide. That was back in 2004, and since then, Hg2 has gone on to publish 32 city guides globally, all with the same aim in mind: to offer independent, insiders' advice to intelligent, urbane travellers with a taste for fine design, good food, the perfect Martini, and a city's inside track. Our take on hedonism is not just about pedal-to-the-metal partying, but a respect for the finer things in life.

Unlike many other guidebooks, we pride ourselves on our independence and integrity. We eat in all the restaurants, drink in all the bars, and go wild in all the nightclubs – all totally incognito. We charge no-one for the privilege of appearing in the guide, refuse print advertising, and include every place at our own discretion. With teams of knowing, on-the-ground contacts, we cover all the scenes but the tourist trap scene – from the establishment to the underground, from bohemia to the plutocrats' playgrounds, from fetish to fashiony drag, and all the places between and beyond, including the commercial fun factories and the neighbourhood institutions. We then present our findings in a clean, logical layout and a photograph accompanying every review, to make your decision process a quick, and effective one, so you can just get amongst what suits you best. Even the books' design is discreet, so as to avoid the dreaded 'hapless tourist' look.

Updates

Hg2 has developed a network of journalists in each city to review the best new hotels, restaurants, bars, clubs, etc, and to keep track of the latest openings. To access our free updates as well as the digital content of each guide, simply log onto our website www.Hg2.com and register. We welcome your help. If you have any comments or recommendations, please feel free to email us at info@hg2.com.

About the Writers

Tristan Rutherford

At the age of five Tristan moved from the Bahamas to the British Midlands. He redressed this seismic shock over the following two decades, visiting 50 countries before the age of 25. After a degree in Politics and Arabic he hounded easyJet magazine for his first commission and has been a travel writer ever since. His work now appears in the FT, The Daily Telegraph and the Sunday Times Travel Magazine. He also lectures in travel journalism at Central Saint Martins in London and Bilgi University in Istanbul. Tristan has been visiting the crossroads of Europe and Asia since 1995 and feels most at home in the fish restaurants of Karaköy and the nargile cafés near the Süleymaniye mosque.

Kathryn Tomasetti

US-born, Italian-raised Kathryn Tomasetti writes travel stories and guidebooks for the likes of The Guardian and The Times. Her library of travel photos – snapped from as far afield as China, Syria and Chile – have been published by Time Out, Dorling Kindersley and The Independent. Kathryn has hunted down archeological ruins and nuggets of culinary knowledge throughout Turkey, often travelling by the country's magical sleeper trains. But Istanbul remains her personal highlight, and she urges visitors to take in the Egyptian Bazaar and the street markets of Kadikoy, as well as the more famous Grand Bazaar.

Istanbul

For much of human history it has been the greatest city on earth. Byzantium, Constantinople, Istanbul – the names by which the city has been known during its 28 centuries of existence are enough alone to conjure such a wealth of legends and stories as to stupefy the most curious of visitors. In that time it played various cameo roles in the great sweeps of ancient history before moving centre-stage as the capital of, successively, two of the world's most powerful empires. Between Constantine's redefinition of the city in AD 330 as the New Rome and the final wreck of the Ottoman Empire in World War I, 97 Latin and Byzantine emperors and empresses and 30 Ottoman sultans ruled their lands from within its walls.

Rumours of the city's splendours, which exhausted the superlatives of the most flowery of high Ottoman poets ('Stambul, peerless of cities, thou jewel beyond compare') have always attracted outsiders. Some came without invitation – the city was seriously besieged 22 times by assorted Greeks, Romans, Franks, Persians, Avars, Slavs, Arabs and Turks. Others, drawn to its centre from the vast imperial peripheries, settled to create the world's first truly cosmopolitan city. For adventurous Europeans from Lord Byron to Pierre Loti, meanwhile, the place was a summation of the exotic attractions of the Orient. For them, like Venice, it was a city to be approached by water from which vantage could be seen, if the timing was right, an otherworldly silhouette of minarets and domes set against a chromatic sunset.

Though the flow of visitors never ceased, the last century was not kind to Istanbul. The City of Cities faded a little from the world's collective memory. But now there are serious signs of revival, not least as a volley of ancient sights were renovated and new museums inaugurated as part of the European Capital of Culture 2010 celebrations.

The city has quadrupled in size over the last few decades as Anatolians have migrated westward in search of betterment in the big city. Of more interest to the visitor, however, will be the hip, contemporary edge that a new generation of young, wealthy Istanbullus have conjured. Slick restaurants replete with cool quadrilingual serving staff serve up new-fangled fusions such as wasabi beef cheeks on a bed of soba noodles while around the corner homegrown classics such as *hunkar begendi* are made with ingrained expertise in eateries that flourished while the sultans still ruled. Meanwhile electronic acts from Berlin or Buenos Aires play to heaving crowds in clubs next door to venues playing Turkish folk.

In what is a hallmark of the greatest cities, Istanbul offers a vibrant present set within a captivating past and visitors are advised to neglect neither.

A few last words by way of introduction – get (mildly) lost (walking). In such a large and, at times, chaotic city, a guidebook, such as this one, should prove invaluable. But if you're unfamiliar with the city, clear a day, head for the middle of the Old City of Sultanahmet, put away your maps and guidebooks, and just wander. After one such walk, though history does not record whether he got lost or not, Lord Byron wrote: 'I have seen the ruins of Athens, of Ephesus, and Delphi. I have traversed great part of Turkey, and many other parts of Europe, and some of Asia; but I never beheld a work of nature or art, which yielded an impression like the prospect on each side from the Seven Towers to the end of the Golden Horn.'

Istanbul

SLEEP

1. A'jia Hotel
2. Edition
3. Sumahan on the Water

EAT

4. Asitane
5. Bebek Balikci
6. Beyti
7. Çiya
8. Develi
9. Kordon Balik
10. Mia Mensa
11. Sunset Grill
12. Ulus 29
13. Zuma

DRINK

14. Bebek Hotel Bar
15. Hush
16. Isis

SNACK

18. Aşşk Kahve
19. Cafe di Dolce
20. Mangerie
21. Pierre Loti Cafe

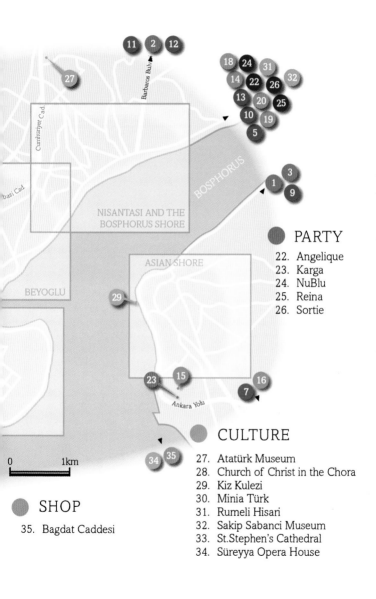

PARTY

22. Angelique
23. Karga
24. NuBlu
25. Reina
26. Sortie

CULTURE

27. Atatürk Museum
28. Church of Christ in the Chora
29. Kiz Kulezi
30. Minia Türk
31. Rumeli Hisari
32. Sakip Sabanci Museum
33. St.Stephen's Cathedral
34. Süreyya Opera House

SHOP

35. Bagdat Caddesi

0   1km

■ Sultanahmet

This neighbourhood is the ancient city, a spit of land bounded by water to the north, south and east, and to the west by the walls built by Theodosius II in the 5th century to keep out the invading hordes. Now a ruined and largely forgotten series of punctuation marks in the city's landscape, the walls protected the Byzantines for a thousand years until, in 1453, Mehmet the Conqueror breached them and claimed it as the capital of the Ottoman Empire.

There are few places in the world where the relics of history are more concentrated or more astonishing than within this circumscribed area. Accordingly, a tourist trail centuries-old connects its great mosques, museums, bazaars and palaces. Disdain for conventional sightseeing aside, they are a must.

Most of Istanbul's unmissable sights are to be found in the Sultanahmet area, the eastern portion of the old city. Supremely famous, and lying at its heart, is the Hagia Sophia, Church of Divine Wisdom, for a millennium the largest building on earth. Its vast, apparently miraculously unsupported dome and spacious interior profoundly impressed Ottoman architects who answered with the Sultanahmet Mosque (also known as the Blue Mosque), its immediate neighbour, and the great Süleymaniye Mosque, which lies a kilometre away to the northwest. Together the three buildings dominate the spectacular skyline. Less vertical, but no less impressive, the Topkapı, palace of sultans for some 400 years and byword for the mystique and baroque

splendour of Oriental majesty, sits on a promontory overlooking the confluence of the Golden Horn and the Bosphorus. Its secrets and treasures are now offered up for global consumption. Delicately ornamented helmets and shields, and jewel-encrusted daggers and chests full of gemstones fill spot lit cases in the Treasury, while an additional ticket grants admission to the Harem, a steamy inner sanctum where once only few could enter without fearing death.

Added to this are museums of archaeology, mosaics and Islamic arts, the ruins of the Hippodrome, obelisks and columns, cisterns and aqueducts, jewel-like churches and elegant mosques, all combining to create a fantasy-like world that's firmly rooted in the past.

Successfully puncturing those dreamlike reveries, however, are the usual tourism-spawned irritations of naff cafés, tourist-tat touts and sleazy salesmen that infest the Sultanahmet area and that other great tourist magnet that lies to its west, the Kapalı Carsi, or Grand Bazaar. But this is an essential Istanbul experience, and visitors can be comforted in the knowledge that locals as well tourists throng its myriad streets in search of a bargain or two.

The effects of the tourist trade also mean that, perversely, unlike the rest of Istanbul, there are only a handful of good restaurants in the area and even fewer drinking or partying spots, confirming the old city as primarily a zone of cultural attractions. But when they are this splendid only the churlish would complain.

13

Sultanahmet

● SLEEP

1. Ayasofya Konaklari
2. Empress Zoe
3. Eresin Crown
4. Four Seasons at Sultanahmet
5. Ibrahim Pasha Hotel
6. Kybele Hotel

● EAT

7. Balikci Sabahattin
8. Hamdi
9. Kumkapi Meyhanes
10. Pandeli
11. Seasons Restaurant

● DRINK

12. Sultan Pub
13. Yesil Ev Beer Garden

● SNACK

17. Erenler Aile Çay Bahçesi
18. The Four Seasons
19. Meşale Çay Bahçesi

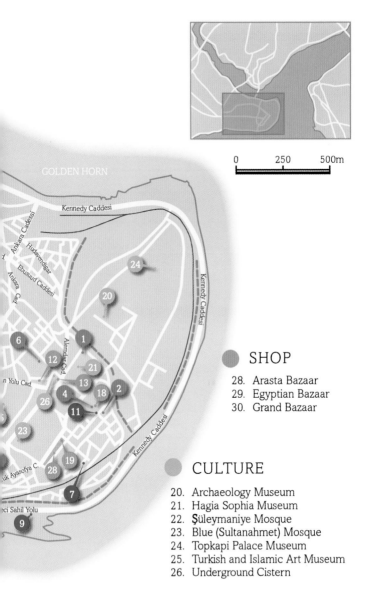

0   250   500m

SHOP

28. Arasta Bazaar
29. Egyptian Bazaar
30. Grand Bazaar

CULTURE

20. Archaeology Museum
21. Hagia Sophia Museum
22. Şüleymaniye Mosque
23. Blue (Sultanahmet) Mosque
24. Topkapi Palace Museum
25. Turkish and Islamic Art Museum
26. Underground Cistern

■ Beyoğlu

Beyoğlu has always been the racier, modern and outré counterpart to the fading, stately and traditional grandeur of Sultanahmet. The area of Galata, just over the Golden Horn, was even in the days of Byzantium the home of foreign workers and merchants. On Galata Bridge the celebrated 19th-century Italian travel writer Edmondo de Amicis observed the parade of people who made up the Ottoman world – Albanians, Armenians, Africans, Jews, Tartars and Turks – and called them 'a changing mosaic of races and religions, that is composed and scattered continually with a rapidity that the eye can scarcely follow'.

In late Ottoman times the area of Pera, north of Galata, took shape, where ambitious Europeans set up hotels, notably the Pera Palace, and embassies such as Charles Barry's neoclassical British Consulate. It was here that electricity, telephony and the general trappings of modernity crash-landed into the hidebound Ottoman world. Their allure proved irresistible and in the mid-19th century the sultans implicitly acknowledged the shift of power, abandoned the Topkapı and built a succession of palaces along the nearby Bosphorus shore. Beyoğlu's great artery, the Grand Rue de Pera (renamed Istiklal Caddesi in the early days of the Turkish Republic), was then a parade of European culture and manners, while in the backstreets a more louche and bohemian atmosphere reigned, fuelled by a concoction of artists, dancers, prostitutes, pimps, writers and spies. When people wax lyrical about the cosmopolitan charms of old Constantinople, it is late-19th-century and early- to mid-20th-century Pera that is at the forefront of their minds, with the melancholy relics of Old Stamboul forming a picturesque backdrop.

The area retained that character up until the 1950s, when an upsurge in Turkish nationalism convinced most minorities to leave. That's now distant history and Beyoğlu is increasingly home to a kaleidoscope of nations, from Greek students and American writers to Iraqi immigrants and Nigerian businessmen. Istiklal Caddesi is now the city's Oxford Street or Boulevard Haussmann, the beautiful 19th-century façades of its buildings dotted by hoardings and neon lights. Off its length run streets that are home to innumerable and wonderful cafés, bars, restaurants, music venues and clubs, many open until the early hours of the morning.

Asmalımescit, westwards off the bottom end of Istiklal, is a particular hotspot that has benefited from artist-led gentrification, with some of the best restaurants in town sitting beside a selection of cool bars and the city's top dance and music club, Babylon, round the corner. Similarly, the neighbouring areas of Çukurcuma and Cihangir, on the other side of Istiklal, are riding high on a property price boom thanks to the creative types who have brought them credibility. Here the bars and restaurants are particularly fashionable, nodal points of an exclusive local social scene. Further north up Istiklal, Çicek Pasajı, one of the many attractive passages that run off the main thoroughfare, is filled with smart waiters dying to lure you into their admittedly charmingly-appointed restaurants. Better, however, to avoid their touristy slickness and turn the corner to experience the rough 'n' ready attractions of the fish market and its adjacent stretch of *meyhanes* (taverns), Nevizade Sokak, both overflowing with the exuberant energy of street life. At its northern conclusion Istiklal finally empties out into the large and largely unappealing expanse of Taksim Square, a suitably symbolic separation, perhaps, between the many joys of Beyoğlu and the business district beyond.

17

Beyoğlu

EAT

8. La Brise
9. Changa
10. Çok Çok
11. Doga Balik
12. Galata House
13. Haci Abdullah
14. Karaköy Lokantasi
15. Karaköy Fish Markets
16. Lokanta Maya
17. Mimolett
18. Nevizade Sokak
19. Refik
20. Tokyo
21. Yakup 2

DRINK

22. 360°
23. 5 Kat
24. Badehane
25. Büyük Londra Hotel Bar
26. Ceyazir
27. Galata Bridge Bars
28. Gizil Bahce
29. The James Joyce
30. K.V.
31. Kino Gardens
32. Lebi-i-Derya
33. Limonlu Bahçe
34. Lokal
35. Nu Terras
36. Pia
37. Sensus Turkish Wine Library
38. Urban

SLEEP

1. Büyük Londra Hotel
2. L'Zaz
3. Marmara Pera
4. Pera Palace
5. Richmond Hotel
6. Tom Tom Suites
7. Witt Suites

SHOP

CULTURE

SNACK

PARTY

Tarlabasi Caddesi
Istikal Caddesi
Sıraselviler Caddesi
Kazancı Yokusu
Mebusan Caddesi
Defterdar Yokusu
Meclisi Mebusan Caddesi
Bogaz Kesen Caddesi
Necatibey Caddesi
Kemankes Caddesi
BOSPHORUS

■ Nisantası & the Bosphorus Shore

North and northeast of Beyoğlu lie the lands of Istanbul's haute bourgeoisie and the playgrounds of the super-rich. The inland area of Nisantası comprises smart streets of modern apartment blocks, fashion boutiques, reassuringly expensive restaurants and people-watching cafés. It doesn't attract too many visitors, who tend to have homegrown versions in their native countries, but it's worth seeing to form a holistic impression of the city that isn't just about fading historical relics. The Beyman Brasserie in the Beyman department store on Abdi Ipekci Caddesi, a leafier and more genteel take on Bond Street or Via Montenapoleone, is an excellent point from which to get the measure of the area. From there you can saunter in and out of the usual slew of designer operations – Gucci, Vuitton, Burberry – plus a host of one-off Turkish boutiques before refreshing yourself at top eateries. In short, Nisantası is a showcase for sleek, modern Istanbul.

The Bosphorus, stretching 14 miles from the Sea of Marmara to the mouth of the Black Sea, is rather more timeless. Its name is mythical: Zeus seduced Io, and so his wife, Hera, took revenge by turning Io into a heifer incessantly tormented by a gadfly. To escape the midge she swam the straits, hence 'Bosphorus' – 'ford of the ox'. Its treacherous currents, which run north–south and vice-versa deep under the surface, are immortalised in the legend of Jason and the Argonauts who famously navigated the channel's vicious, clashing rocks.

More recently, the Bosphorus has been the fantastical playground of the city's elite. It was here that the sultans moved after abandoning the Topkapı, building first the rococo pile that is the Dolmabahçe, the Çıragan Palace, the Beylerbeyi Palace (on the Asian shore) and, finally, Yıldız Palace, which sits on a hillside of lovely woods, ponds and streams just over the road from the Çıragan. Their wealthy subjects, meanwhile, studded the shoreline all the way up to the Black Sea with their *yalı* homes (wooden summer mansions), still some of the world's most expensive properties. All are best seen on the Bosphorus Cruise (see Culture), which breezes past every seafront pad in the city.

Despite, presumably, possessing neither palace nor *yalı*, you can enjoy the Bosphorus at any of the excellent cafés, clubs and restaurants as you journey northwards along its shore. The area of Ortaköy, with its Italian-style piazza, is a trendy hotspot, just south of the kilometre-long Bosphorus Bridge. Kuruçeşme is home to superclubs Reina, Sortie and Anjelique, as well the trendy Aşşk Café and Italian

restaurant Mia Mensa. Further along, Bebek, the loveliest of the Bosphorus villages, as they were before being encompassed by Greater Istanbul, boasts renowned fish restaurant Bebek Balıkçı, a fabulous bar at the back of the stylish Bebek Hotel, and Meşur Bebek Badem Ezmesci purveyors of what may be the finest *badem ezmesci* (marzipan) in the world.

Round the next bend stand icons of antiquity and modernity: the imposing Ottoman castle, Rumeli Hisarı (and on the opposite shore its twin Anadolu Hisarı), and the Fatih Mehmet Bridge, a world-beating suspension bridge linking Europe to Asia. Funnily enough, it's sited exactly where King Darius of Persia built a pontoon bridge in 512 BC so he could attack the Scythians. Just another place where the city's present is in play with its past.

Nisantası &
the Bosphorus Shore

● DRINK
12. Taps

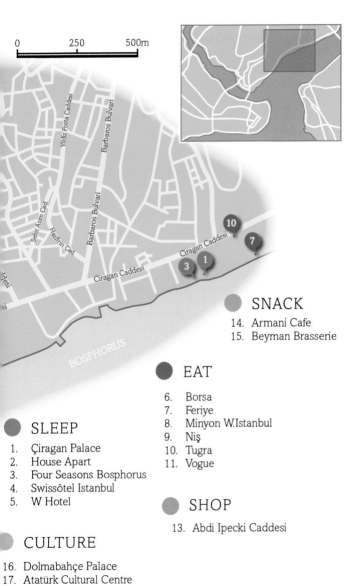

0   250   500m

SNACK

14. Armani Cafe
15. Beyman Brasserie

EAT

6. Borsa
7. Feriye
8. Minyon W.Istanbul
9. Niş
10. Tuğra
11. Vogue

SLEEP

1. Çiragan Palace
2. House Apart
3. Four Seasons Bosphorus
4. Swissôtel Istanbul
5. W Hotel

SHOP

13. Abdi Ipecki Caddesi

CULTURE

16. Dolmabahçe Palace
17. Atatürk Cultural Centre

■ The Asian Shore (Üsküdar/Kadiköy)

When the ancient Greek Byzas asked an oracle where he should found his city, the oracle reputedly said 'opposite the blind', referring to the Chalcedonians who settled on the Asian side of the Bosphorus in the 7th century BC, ignoring the obvious advantages of the European shore. Perhaps they just wanted a quieter life. A 20-minute boat trip from the teeming attractions of the European to the Asian shore indeed offers visitors a taste of Turkish life at a calmer pace, as well as the chance to boast you've crossed continents to find it.

It is only in the last two decades that the collection of villages on the Asian side of the Bosphorus has found themselves caught up in the mushroom-like growth of the city and recast as suburbs. The two main areas are Uskudar to the north, which faces Beyoğlu across the water, and south, Üsküdar, opposite the Old City area of Sultanahmet. Despite their wealth of mosques and markets these districts don't attract too many tourists. That doesn't stop locals flocking to the massive Salı Pazarı Tuesday market, just a short bus ride from Kadıköy. Closer to the neighbourhood's ferry terminal is Çiya, a wonderfully unpretentious restaurant given the quality of its Anatolian cooking and in itself a destination worthy of the ferry trip. And with overcrowding across the straits, a number of hip drinking holes have relocated their business here – including Hush and 360°.

Wandering up the shore to Üsküdar takes you past the Kız Kulesi – Maiden's Tower – an immensely popular landmark and the scene of M's incarceration in the Bond flick *The World Is Not Enough*. Located just offshore on its own rocky outcrop and accessible only by boat it is nonetheless a good place for a coffee and a pleasant spot from which to look at the Bosphorus. Round the bend is the beautiful Şemsi Pasa Mosque, one of the smallest, by star Ottoman architect Mimar Sinan.

24

You may wish to travel further afield as a trip to the Asian shore often awakes impulses to escape and explore (particularly after the intensity of the European parts of Istanbul). One route northwards takes in the Asian Bosphorus villages, of which Kanlıca is one of the most charming, famous since the 17th-century for its thick yoghurts. Further north is Çengelköy, famed this time for its tasty cucumbers and the stupendously good fish restaurant, Kordon Balık. Sleeping in this tranquil zone is also possible – the chilled confines of Sumahan on the Water and A'Jia offer sanctuary and sea views, and will buzz passengers into the heart of the action on their private speedboats.

In the other direction, the Prens Adaları – the Princes' Islands – lie off the south coast of Kadıköy. A collection of tranquil islands where superfluous Byzantine princes were once exiled (the more efficient Ottomans tended simply to strangle theirs), they have long attracted ethnically diverse settlers, bourgeois pleasure-seekers from the city and assorted exiles, including, for a while, Leon Trotsky, Edward VIII and Wallace Simpson. But those with more extreme wanderlust need only venture into the idiosyncratically Teutonic form of Haydarpaşa station in Kadıköy, a gift from Kaiser Wilhelm, where you can catch trains for as far east as Tehran.

The Asian Shore
(Üsküdar/Kadiköy)

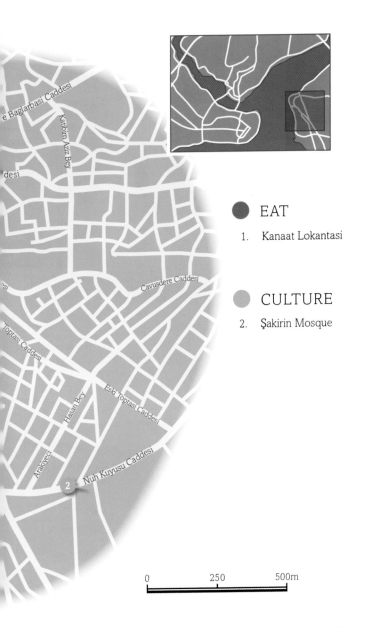

EAT

1. Kanaat Lokantasi

CULTURE

2. Şakirin Mosque

0   250   500m

Istanbul's upcoming neighbourhoods

Mention to most Istanbullus that you're bedding down in Beyoğlu or Karaköy and you'll receive a weak smile. It's no longer considered bizarre for a wealthy foreigner to choose a hotel in a tumbledown area of town, but why you'd spurn the luxuries of the new airport Hilton is utterly beyond them. For a real neighbourhood snobbery test mention that you'd like to meet your local host in Asmalımescit. The thought of this raucously warren-like jumble of bars and discos will be met with the polite compliance of someone who'd rather show you a more modern side of town. Just a decade ago Asmalımescit's main income was derived from hookers, smugglers and flophouse hotels. Reputations die hard.

But times are changing. A perfect storm of strident economic growth and new values placed on glorious old real estate has swept over Istanbul's crumbling bourgeois neighbourhoods. The regular economy rode up by 8% per year in 2010 and 2011 with the service and creative industry buzzing along at an extra gear. The city's stock of Italian-built palazzi, Frenchy townhouses and huge Gothic terraces have become the backdrop for the city's coolest clubs, shops, restaurants and hotels.

It takes a generation of wealth to appreciate the concept of shabby chic. It's now the vogue for Istanbul's jeunesse dorée to party on the parquet wearing vintage Lacoste and second-hand Chanel. Foreign visitors – whose numbers have surged

by a steady 15% per year since 2007 – have unwittingly fuelled the regeneration of both Beyoğlu and Karaköy, plus Beşiktaş and Taksim too. The dearth of accommodation in the edgiest areas of town has sprouted a new generation of boutique B&Bs (like I'Zaz), aparthotels (like The House Apart) and small historic hotels (like TomTom) in the areas that the big hotel brands just can't reach. The same was true in New York's Brooklyn or London's Notting Hill in the 1990s. Even Harlem and Hackney are now on the radar for a splash of urban cool.

In tandem to the once seedier areas of London, Barcelona or Sydney, prices have shot through the roof too. A case in point is the neighbourhood of Galata. This maze of second-hand stores and boutique B&Bs borders bourgeois Beyoğlu and the former docklands of Karaköy. In the 1990s it was not so much 'no-go' as 'no-thank-you'. Half the zone's predominately Italianate building stock – think marble staircases and moulded ceilings – were derelict, while the rest was blackened by neglect. A penthouse apartment here with views across the Bosphorus would have cost ten thousand euros. Fast-forward a decade and the same flat is worth half a million, a sum only limited by a temporary embargo on foreigners purchasing local property. Rental fees have become sillier still. Properties that recently let for a few hundred lira a month are currently being offered for a thousand euros per week. Those who took a punt on a property here now have a healthy second income and wear a look of unmitigated joy.

On the flipside of such upwardly mobile aspirations is the neighbourhood of Tarlabaşı. Its housing stock mirrors that of Galata, but the location has been hitherto on the wrong side of the boulevard below Taksim, and its passage to gentrification has been a stormy one. A strong community spirit prevails in the mostly immigrant Anatolian and Kurdish community, with chatter passing from window to window. Baskets of groceries are still hauled up from street level from passing carts. New arrivals are welcome too. Istanbul's large transvestite and transsexual community has found a home here, as have an arty crowd priced out of the city's up-and-already-came neighbourhoods. But not everybody understands the ethos of urban regeneration. Rough and ready Tarlabaşı is now on the receiving end of a top-down municipal renewal project. Eviction notices have been served, and the zone is soon to be mostly demolished in order to make way for high-density, high-value new-build housing.

Tarlabaşı aside, many of Istanbul's changing neighbourhoods make for an exciting visit. Areas that were once unseemly now offer the most authentic and architecturally splendid view of everyday Istanbul. There are several new holiday rental options in the old Greek neighbourhood of Fener, which abuts the Golden Horn. Here ancient Ottoman houses lie tangled in jasmine and bougainvillea, while a street market – think car boot sale meets Portobello Road – takes over the (recently) UNESCO-protected neighbourhood each Sunday.

Across the Galata Bridge, Bankalar Caddesi has gone from commercial dead-end to cultural hub in the last few years. A stroll down the hill brings visitors past the freshly renovated and impossibly grand mansions of the colonial banks. The newly signposted Komando steps (an M.C. Escher style passageway) are also here, as is the grand SALT Galata art space, which opened for business in November 2011.

Other historical areas to explore include Kumkapı, which runs along the Sea of Marmara. This old Greek neighbourhood is punctuated with a volley of Orthodox and Armenian churches plus a string of top fish restaurants. In the past year or two the former Latin area of Feriköy with its old Catholic graveyard has been touted as the new Galata, which was once, of course, the new Cihangir, which is turn was the new Nişantaşı. Wherever next?

31

sleep...

Istanbul's hotel scene was once a staid collection of big-brand hotels and rough 'n' ready local joints. Over the past few years the introduction of suite-only concepts, a rash of über-hip design hotels and several renovated palatial showstoppers have delivered a range of accommodation that's nothing short of revolutionary. So keen is the competition to create the city's most sumptuous, most eclectic or most avant-garde that the lobbies and bars of many of our recommendations are worth a visit in their own right.

There is no such thing as the perfect place to stay. Istanbul is a large city and can be time-consuming to traverse, so you should select accommodation to suit your primary need, be it shopping, history, R&R or a mix of all three. Visitors who wish to immerse themselves primarily in the historical sights will naturally want to stay in the Sultanahmet area, within walking distance of the Blue Mosque, Grand Bazaar and Topkapı Palace. The Empress Zoe, the Ibrahim Pasa Hotel and Eresin Crown offer smart, old-fashioned comfort – indeed the latter has the unique boast of being a museum hotel, exhibiting catalogued items from the Archaeology Museum's collection, including some fabulous busts and columns. Easily the best in show is the Four Seasons at Sultanahmet, a paean to traditional luxury placed – rather unconventionally – inside an old Ottoman prison.

The hotels of the Pera district of Beyoğlu, meanwhile, offer a good compromise for those who wish to be in the midst of Istanbul's buzzing bar and restaurant district while remaining only a short tram or taxi ride away from the sights of the old city. In its centre is the famed Pera Palace, whose Victorian-era glory is once again resplendent after a grand renovation in 2010. Basking in the area's newly cool aura are the Marmara Pera and several well-priced suite-only apartment concepts, include I'zaz and various outposts of The House Apart, another concept hotel where breakfast is served in any of the city's hip House Café branches.

Panning along the seafront from lower Beyoğlu to Besiktas is a volley of utterly opulent design hotels, located for the most part in historical buildings with Bosphorus backdrops. Witt Suites has been picking up design awards since its inception in 2009. TomTom Suites, housed inside an old Franciscan nunnery, has achieved similar acclaim. And the W Hotel – Europe's first – in the old Dolmabahçe Palace stables has been wowing guests with rainforest showers and private gardens (each leading off its deluxe double rooms) since 2008. Beyond the Besiktas football stadium, the new Four Seasons at the Bosphorus welcomes visitors inside an old Ottoman *palazzo*, the venerable Çıragan Palace occupies the country's former parliament and – from late 2012 – the Shangri-La looks out to sea from an impressive old tobacco emporium.

If splendid isolation is more your thing, you may wish to head instead to the Asian shore, where the entrepreneurial Doors Group, owners of a slew of fashionable restaurants and nightclubs, have converted a *yalı*, one of the late-Ottoman wooden mansions that line the Bosphorus, into A'jia, a romantically decorated, 16-room boutique hotel. Similarly, the owners of the highly rated Kordon restaurant have converted an old *raki* distillery into the petite, super-slick Sumahan on the Water.

Given the fluctuations of the Turkish Lira and the cosmopolitan nature of most visitors to the city, hotel prices in Istanbul are listed in Euros. The range given is the price of a standard room during low season to the price of a deluxe double in high season.

the best hotels…

Çiragan Palace

A'jia Hotel *(top)*
Ahmet Rasim Paşa Yalısı,
Çubuklu Caddesi 27, Kanlıca
Tel: 00 90 216 413 9300
www.ajiahotel.com
Rates: €200–340

Opened in summer 2005, A'jia was one of the first design hotels on the Istanbul scene. It remains one of the city's most fabulous, although prices are thankfully a shade lower than some of the more blingy arrivistes. The 16-room establishment occupies a lovely *yalı* (Ottoman wooden mansion) built by Ahmet Rasim Pasa on the Asian shore of the Bosphorus near Kanlıca, a village famous for its creamy yoghurts. Not that Ahmet Rasim Pasa would necessarily feel at home if he were to return. The interior has been given a sleek, contemporary and minimalist overhaul, complete with oh-so-glamorous restaurant. White and beige dominate in the cool communal areas, while it's all about cream furniture and dark wood in the rooms. The hotel's removed location may be either a major attraction or seriously off-putting, depending on your inclination: although you can get to the Old City or Beyoğlu by water (nearby ferry or the hotel's complimentary speedboat), or by taxi over the bridge, it's clearly not an ideal base for efficient sightseeing. Conversely, the hotel is in a zone of calm, modern luxury away from the hectic city, with spectacular views of the Bosphorus.

Style 8, Atmosphere 8, Location 6

Ayasofya Konakları *(middle)*
Sogukçesme Sokak, Sultanhamet
Tel: 00 90 212 513 3660
www.ayasofyapensions.com
Rates: €120–200

There are few hotels in the world that can boast of having three world-class cultural attractions on their doorstep. Most of those spots that can are in Sultanhamet, and the Ayasofya Konakları (Ayasofya Mansions) may trump them all. On an old cobbled lane next door to the Topkapı Palace, just behind the Hagia Sophia and a small, weak child's stone-throw from the Blue Mosque, its location is hard to better. Built in the 1980s by the Turkish Touring and Automobile Association, the Ayasofya Konakları was the first Ottoman boutique hotel. Unusually, it is a row of pretty, pastel-coloured houses, with a total of 57 rooms and seven suites – some looking onto the Hagia Sophia itself – built to mimic exactly the old Ottoman houses that once stood in their place. A separate building in pretty surroundings at the end of the street houses a restaurant and bar. Rooms are decorated with Ottoman-style beds, tables and objets d'art, which range from the stuffy to the chic.

Style 6, Atmosphere 6, Location 9

Büyük Londra Hotel *(bottom)*
Meşrutiyet Caddesi 53, Tepebaşı
Tel: 00 90 212 245 0670
www.londrahotel.net
Rates: €60–120

A serious option for visitors with a restricted budget and/or a developed sense of humour. The Londra is an eccentric survivor of the high Victo-

rian grandeur of Pera and a contemporary of its more glamorous near neighbour, the Pera Palace. A showy, ornate façade, replete with a graceful row of caryatids, is matched for attention by the period interior décor of the lobby. The occasionally raucous bar (it's where Istanbul's foreign correspondents club holds their monthly meets) has elaborate ceilings mouldings, enlivened by rather glaring colour choices that compete for attention with voluptuous chandeliers and loud wallpaper. The (few) staff, meanwhile, are more likely to be playing solitaire on computer than paying attention to anything in particular. Those are the high points. The rooms, though large, range from the threadbare to the unsympathetically renovated, with basic bathrooms throughout. The whole place is slightly reminiscent of those hotels in

India that attempt to maintain the style and etiquette of the days of the Raj on shoestring budgets and only hazy, second-hand recollections of what they were in the first place.

Style 5, Atmosphere 7, Location 6

Çırağan Palace *(left)*
Çırağan Caddesi 32, Beşiktaş
Tel: 00 90 212 326 4646
www.kempinski.com/istanbul
Rates: €510–1,350

Sultan Abdülaziz built the Çırağan Palace in 1874 and committed suicide inside it two years later – possibly because he'd made a mess of his reign, but more probably because he had psychic premonition of the cleaning costs associated with the palace's

magnificently OTT central-tiered atrium (home, incidentally, to the world's heaviest chandelier). The waterside palace became home of the Ottoman Empire's nascent parliament before a major fire ushered in a long period of neglect. Now refitted and run to an extraordinarily high standard by hotel kingmakers Kempinski, amenities include a *hamam*, an amazing outdoor pool that appears to flow into the Bosphorus and several superb restaurants including the award-winning Tuğra (see Eat). Other eateries include the Gazebo Lounge, which serves a highly recommended afternoon tea, and Laledan, which dishes up a stupefyingly rich Sunday Brunch complete with sushi stand and oyster bar. The palace section of the building holds a small history museum and non-guests are invited to wander through. However, a

key code and a Lichtenstein bank account are needed to access the Çırağan's dozen palace suites, which share an additional private lounge and a team of butlers. At 376-square-metres, the Sultan Suite is said to be the third most expensive in Europe. Libya's mini despot Saif al-Gaddhafi was reportedly a regular, but it seems he won't be using the suite's Molton Brown toiletries any time soon.

Style 8, Atmosphere 9, Location 8

Empress Zoe *(right)*
Akbıyık Caddesi 4/1,
Sultanahmet
Tel: 00 90 212 518 2504
www.emzoe.com
Rates: €120–185

Small, stylish, perfectly placed and fairly priced, the Empress Zoe is one of the best options in the Old City for visitors who can't afford or don't want something as expensive or as formal as the Four Seasons. Named after a famous 11th-century Byzantine empress who chomped through a succession of lovers and husbands over her lifetime, the hotel has 22 rooms, which are clean, prettily decorated and uncluttered – handy, because they're a smidge on the small side. You're better off spending time in the romantic, beautiful and leafy back garden, where you can rest and relax amid the ruins of a 15th-century *hamam*. Alternatively, you can dawdle on the rooftop terrace, which has superb views. The hotel is within hailing distance of the local mosque, so bring earplugs unless you fancy waking up with the faithful at dawn.

Style 6, Atmosphere 7, Location 8

Edition *(top)*
Büyükdere Caddesi 136, Levent
Tel: 00 90 212 317-7700
www.editionhotels.com
Rates: €375–750

Istanbul's clamorous hotel industry looked guardedly on when the Edition opened in May 2011. Would its location in business-friendly Levent be too far out? Would the group behind the grand design, Marriot, prove too cost-conscious and conservative? They didn't factor in Ian Schrager, the hotelier behind London's The Sanderson and Miami's Delano, who teamed up with the chain for this new business-class hotel

concept. The 78 rooms, spread over 12 floors, are vast. Each one is refinement personified, with heavy B&O remotes, carved Corian bathrooms and drapes that whiz noiselessly open to reveal the Istanbul skyline at the touch of a button. Schrager's insistent touches are all over the communal areas, too: calves' leather cushions and free coffee in the first floor lounge and Italian Travertine walls in the meeting rooms. An ESPA spa stretches five storeys underground, where a leather floor is soft on the toes, and there's a real-live snow room if you'd like to go Finnish after a steam in the *hamam*. Taksim Square is four speedy stops away on the nearby Metro.

Style 9, Atmosphere 7, Location 5

Eresin Crown *(bottom)*
Küçük Ayasofya Caddesi 40,
Sultanahmet
Tel: 00 90 212 638 4428
www.eresin.com.tr
Rates: €190–250

The Eresin Crown can, uniquely, style itself as a 'boutique museum hotel', because dotted around the 59-roomed property are catalogued items from the Istanbul Archaeology Museum. Happily, this is really just icing on a quality cake that ranks the Eresin Crown among the best luxury hotels in Sultanahmet. The experience of the Eresin family, which runs several hotels in the city, shows itself in the professional levels of service. All the smart, modern rooms have parquet flooring and Jacuzzis. The only letdown is the occasional lapse into kitsch, most criminally in the ground-floor Column Bar, where several ancient columns are inveigled into a somewhat tasteless interior decoration scheme. Several bars and hotels in Sultanahmet have rooftop terraces with incredible views, including the Eresin Crown, but in fortuitous continuity with its antiquarian theme the hotel's rooftop terrace restaurant and bar offers, in addition, a unique perspective on the substructure of the Hippodrome. The Blue Mosque is a stiff ten-minute uphill hike away.

Style 6, Atmosphere 7, Location 7

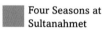

Four Seasons at *(top)*
Sultanahmet
Tevkifhane Sokak 1, Sultanahmet
Tel: 00 90 212 402 3000
www.fourseasons.com/istanbul
Rates: €480–610

The most luxurious traditional hotel in Istanbul (unless you're forking out for the palace suites in the Çiragan), the Four Seasons has been a hit (especially with wealthy Americans) since its opening in 1994. Originally the building it occupies was an Ottoman prison built to service the nearby courts of law: both Turkish author Yaşara Kemal and controversial poet Nazım Hikmet were imprisoned here. Standards of service have considerably improved since those days, an irony that the original inmates would no doubt have enjoyed. The building's history has inadvertently bequeathed the hotel a kind of Ottoman minimalism, with distinctive features such as pointed arches and tall ceilings uncomplicated by the Turkish tendency towards the baroque

(prisoners were not deemed worthy of baroque visual excitement). The 65 large rooms are full of opulent furnishings, as well as contemporary fittings like iPod docks and so on. The location, between the Hagia Sophia and the Blue Mosque, is a history-lover's dream; the Seasons Restaurant is one of the best places in town to sample sophisticated European and Turkish regional cuisine, plus there's a killer Sunday brunch to soak up a Saturday night drinking session. And as of 2011, a clever, traffic-evading water taxi link has been installed to allow guests to zip along the Bosphorus between the Four Seasons' two Istanbul locations. Inevitably, top rates are charged for what is a top product.

Style 8, Atmosphere 8, Location 9

Four Seasons *(bottom)*
at the Bosphorus
Çırağan Caddesi 28, Beşiktaş
Tel: 00 90 212 381 4000
www.fourseasons.com/bosphorus
Rates: €480–610

Istanbul received a pat on the back when it achieved the accolade of being the only city in mainland Europe to boast two Four Seasons: the luxury brand's second sumptuous hotel was built on the banks of the Bosphorus in 2008. It remains more amenity-rich and business-like than its sister hotel in Sultanahmet, with many guests booking a two-centre Istanbul old 'n' new experience (the hotel is happy to shuttle you and your bags by speedboat between the two). The 150 guestrooms and suites are contemporary Ottoman

– think sofas and art alaturka but nothing too outlandish, and be aware that not all rooms overlook the Bosphorus. Suites are a step up, with high ceilings and hardwood floors. The three-bedroom Atik Pasha suite is a 375-square-metrre fun palace with potentate pretensions. It's the communal areas that separate this hotel from the row of five-star hotels in Beşiktaş. Several *hamams* and spa zones line the city's largest indoor swimming pool, and outside there's another massive pool surrounded by Ottoman gazebos and sun loungers.

Style 8, Atmosphere 7, Location 7

Ibrahim Pasha Hotel *(left)*
Terzihane Sokak 7, Sultanahmet
Tel: 00 90 212 518 0394
www.ibrahimpasha.com
Rates: €185–245

One of the best small hotels in Sultanahmet, the Ibrahim Pasa Hotel is an old, four-storey, late Ottoman house given a thorough, contemporary going-over. Tastefully, the management has neither ruined the period feel of the building by trying too hard nor omitted to add contemporary features. A cosy fireplace and well-worn leather sofa greets guests on entrance. The dozen standard and dozen deluxe rooms may

be modern but each one has enough Sultanahmet kookiness to let you know you're around the corner from both the Hagia Sophia and the Topkapı Palace – many have weird slopey ceilings and cracking views over town. Attractively-tiled and patterned floors set the visual tone throughout, highlighted by the odd bit of statuary or large ornamental pot. The roof terrace overlooking the Blue Mosque is absolutely spectacular.

Style 5, Atmosphere 7, Location 8

....

| **I'Zaz** | *(right)* |

Balık Sokak 12, Beyoğlu

Tel: 00 90 212 252 1382
www.izaz.com
Rates: €70–90

Zeynep Özçelik returned from an eight-year stint in Hollywood with a kooky hotel concept. She devised a suite-only guesthouse where young creatives – be they movie directors, designers or writers – could work in luxurious privacy with a lightning-fast WiFi connection and an in-room coffee machine. The model has certainly caught on. Some guests have stayed a month or more, and the chatter in the communal rooftop kitchen-cum-bar centres around the city's latest exhibitions, art house films et al. Despite neighbouring the old British Embassy – now the UK's Consulate-General – the area remained rough 'n' ready until long after the millennium, with I'zaz a derelict townhouse until Zeynep purchased it. She placed a suite on each of the four floors, connected by a cast-iron spiral staircase with a brushed brick backdrop. Rooms are accessed by keycode, and each has a tidy shower room and an Ottoman-style bay window boudoir for checking out the colourful street life below.

Style 8, Atmosphere 6, Location 6

The House Apart *(left)*
various locations in Tünel,
Galatasaray and Nişantaşi
Tel: 00 90 212 244 3400
www.thehouseapart.com
Rates: €75–150

A slick concept from The House Café – purveyors of a dozen superb restaurants in the trendiest areas of town – is this apart-hotel scheme. All in all around 30 cute, fully-equipped apartments are dotted throughout Istanbul's most atmospheric neighbourhoods where the big-brand hotels just can't reach. Apartments vary in styles – many with parquet floors, some with whacking great terraces – and range from 30- to 60-square-metres in size. Don't expect designer luxury, but all locations come complete with fast WiFi, soft linen and a kitchen large enough to bust out a mean *imam bayildi.* It's the other perks that really offer value, especially for the price. All guests receive complimentary access to the city's hi-tech Mac gyms and a belly-busting daily breakfast in any branch of the House Café.

Style 6, Atmosphere 7, Location 9

Kybele Hotel *(top)*
Yerebatan Caddesi 35,
Sultanahmet
Tel: 00 90 212 511 7766
www.kybelehotel.com
Rates: €120

This small hotel – run by the friendly Akbaryrak family and found just up the road from the Hagia Sophia and the Blue Mosque – distinguishes itself from the myriad of other small Istanbul hotels by its charming weirdness. The bright turquoise, yellow and purple exterior colour scheme sets the tone and is best observed, glass of tea in-hand, from the leafy hotel garden. Inside and throughout the hotel hang thousands of coloured-glass Turkish lamps, which can be found in any of the bazaars, the high point of a decidedly maximalist interior design, with armchairs, sofas and antiques of various periods all vying for attention. A small, very red, pink and ornate lounge area with original late 19th-century features is particularly eye-catching. The Kybele's 16 rooms are moderately-sized, but they have lovely en-suite bathrooms and plenty of coloured lighting.

Style 6, Atmosphere 6, Location 7

Marmara Pera *(right)*
Meşrutiyet Caddesi 1, Tepebaşi
Tel: 00 90 212 334 0300
www.themarmarahotels.com
Rates: €170–210

Occupying a renovated 1970s tower block slap-bang in the centre of old Pera, views from the Marmara Pera take in three or four million lesser mortals at a glance. Inside post-minimalist interior design has something of the Ian Schrager about it, with the odd ornate touch, such as a crystal chandelier or 1970s-style coloured leather chair, offsetting a predominantly dark colour scheme and spacious environment. The hotel's size – at 200 rooms – is just small enough to ensure you don't get a sense of being anonymously swamped, which is common in Istanbul's larger luxury hotels. But two big bonuses high above the skyline mark the Marmara Pera out from the crowd: the first is the astonishing rooftop pool with its wooden surround, reserved exclusively for hotel guests; the second is the super-

cool Mikla winebar and restaurant on the floor below, which serves up excellent fusion cuisine, priceless panoramas and pricey drinks to match.

Style 7, Atmosphere 6, Location 7

Pera Palace *(left)*
Meşrutiyet Caddesi 52, Tepebaşı
Tel: 00 90 212 377 4000
www.perapalace.com
Rates: €185–475

To stay in the Pera Palace rather than the equally luxurious Çırağan Palace or Four Seasons is to value this hotel's unique historical significance. Built by the owners of the Orient Express and designed by French architect Alexander Vallaury, the hotel has, since 1891,

48

allowed a host of the rich, famous and regal to shack up under its roof. Guests have included King Edward VIII, various Shahs and more arms dealers, crooks and spies than the CIA informants' budget. Like Istanbul itself, the hotel went through a deep depression and its threadbare soul limped on until 2007, with only the *garçon, monsieur* and *concierge* buttons by each bar stool testament to its former grandeur (not that any of them worked, of course). But in late 2010 the Pera Palace reopened after a magisterial overhaul, its soul and its ancient cage lift (the city's first elevator) still very much intact. Anecdotal evidence of past times from Orient Express ticket stubs to menus from the roaring '20s are sealed in glass display cabinets on each of the six floors. Period furniture resides in every guestroom, while the six Greta Garbo corner suites are timelessly elegant and way larger than their pre-renovation incarnation. Room 414, where Agatha Christie allegedly penned Murder on the Orient Express, commemorates her stays en-route to the Orient from 1926 to 1932. A *haman*, spa and swimming pool in the sub-basement level are welcome new additions.

Style 8, Atmosphere 9, Location 7

....

Richmond Hotel　　*(right)*
İstiklal Caddesi 227, Beyoğlu
Tel: 00 90 212 252 5460
www.richmondhotels.com.tr
Rates: €135–215

With　　decent-sized　　contemporary

rooms, an expansive lobby, bar and a rooftop restaurant with outstanding views of Sultanahmet and the Bosphorus, plus professional levels of service, the Richmond is a high-quality, if slightly characterless accommodation option. Crucially, however, it's the only hotel on the entire length of İstiklal Caddesi, the pedestrianised artery of Beyoğlu. Located towards İstiklal's southern end, the Richmond is only a short walk away from many of Beyoğlu's hotspots, including the *meyhane*-packed Asmalı Mescit district, which is just over the road. It's also close to Galata, where you can hop in a cab for the short ride to the Old City: ideal for visitors planning to split their time between sightseeing and experiencing Istanbul's more contemporary pleasures.

Style 5, Atmosphere 6, Location 8

....

Sumahan on the Water *(top)*
Kuleli Caddesi 51, Çengelköy
Tel: 00 90 216 422 8000
www.sumahan.com
Rates: €175–325

Opened in May 2005, Sumahan on the Water is a fantastically stylish renovation of an old building on the Asian shore of the Bosphorus. The Sumahan was formerly a 19th-century Ottoman distillery that made *raki*, eventually purchased by the present owner's grandfather. Consequently, the hotel has the kind of spaciousness and cool aesthetic common to converted industrial buildings in London and New York but rare in Istanbul. The renovation is superb and the 20 design rooms each have lovely Bosphorus views, modern fireplaces, fashionable furniture and

all entertainment and communication mod-cons. There are 13 very spacious suites; a number of them are duplexes boasting their own petite terrace gardens where you can sit on the lawn and enjoy the vista. Downstairs is Kordon, an excellent fish restaurant belonging to the same owner. As with A'jia, the location could be either a dream or a hassle. Though the hotel's private launch will whisk you across the Bosphorus to Kabataş on the European side in 15 minutes, or you can hop in a cab into town – a 30-minute ride – from the hotel's front door.

Style 8, Atmosphere 7, Location 6

....

Swissôtel Istanbul *(bottom)*
– The Bosphorus
Bayıldım Caddesi 2, Maçka
Tel: 00 90 212 326 1100
www.swissotel.com/istanbul
Rates: €230–360

Swissôtel celebrated its 20th anniversary in 2011 but it's still scooping up awards for luxury and service, if not cutting-edge design. This big-brand establishment is also a hotel of choice for low-key potentates and visiting royalty – the more blingtastic of sovereigns prefer the Çırağan Palace or the Four Seasons. Swissôtel is located just up from the water on a wooded hilltop, and many of its 500 five-star rooms boast truly magnificent skyline views over the Bosphorus. Amenities include 14 different restaurants, Turkish baths, spas, saunas, fitness centres, an indoor pool, tennis courts, a jogging path (extremely rare in the city), etc. Be aware that this enviable list of comforts is housed in a luxuriously anonymous

hotel where the usual chintzy interior abounds; the marble décor throughout leads to the assumption that several marble quarries have quite possibly been emptied to fit out the hotel.

Style 7, Atmosphere 7, Location 7

TomTom Suites *(left)*
Boğazkesen Caddesi. Tomtom Kaptan Sokak 18, Beyoğlu
Tel: 0212 292 4949
www.tomtomsuites.com
Rates: €200–250

TomTom isn't just a delightfully tasteful suite-only hotel, it's also one that best describes the Beyoğlu area's riches-to-rags-to-riches tale. This Frenchified district was once awash with churches, embassies and merchants' homes, and TomTom started life as a French law court annex before becoming a Franciscan nunnery. After a period of neglect, it reopened in 2008 as an art-filled boutique hotel run by an experienced manager, Mr. Celal, and his deferential staff. Suites are refined and comfortable, not over-designed or loud. Each has a whacking great bathroom lined with Carrara marble, with a freestand-

ing Jacuzzi-bath as a chic centrepiece. Breakfast is one of the best in the business, with village cheeses from across Turkey and homemade preserves. The morning's news can be read on one of the half-dozen hotel iPads that are dished out to each table. Sunset drinks and dinner in the rooftop restaurant, La Mouette, are heartily recommended. Nighttime serenity – and security – is assured by the location of the Italian Consulate General across the road.

Style 8, Atmosphere 8, Location 7

Witt Suites *(right)*
Defterdar Yokusu 26, Cihangir
Tel: 00 90 212 293 1500
www.designhotels.com/witt_istanbul
Rates: €179–499

This intoxicatingly gorgeous hotel is testament to what happens when you give a design team carte blanche over the interiors. In this case the designers were Autoban – Istanbul's avant-garde architect firm – and boy did the company spend some money. The hotel is made up of 17 sumptuous suites – there are no puny 'deluxe doubles' in this establishment. The minimum suite

53

size is a whopping 60-square-metres, although many are much larger with Bosphorus views to boot: little wonder Witt won Wallpaper* magazine's best new hotel award in 2009. The free-standing kitchenettes in the middle of each suite are an immediate showstopper, made of Turkish marble and holding just enough equipment to blend a killer piña colada. Witt also benefits from a 1:1 staff-to-client ratio, a bar that serves a complimentary home-cooked breakfast, and a library stocked with design tomes and the sort of intelligent novels that you are supposed to read but never get around to. Prices are nevertheless keen compared with the city's other upscale offerings.

Style 10, Atmosphere 8, Location 7

....

 W Hotel *(right)*
Süleyman Seba Caddesi 22,
Beşiktaş
Tel: 00 90 212 381 2121
www.wistanbul.com.tr
Rates: €305–475

This outpost of the über-hip W Hotel brand – Europe's first – neatly symbolises Istanbul's rise from bankrupt aristocrat to the continent's coolest city. Housed inside the old stables and dormitories of the nearby Dolmabahçe palace, the W's 136 guestrooms loop around the high-end stores of the Akaretler neighbourhood, among them Marc Jacobs, Marni and Jimmy Choo. Accommodation starts with 30m^2 Wonderful rooms, which boast rainforest showers and Bose sound systems. Spectacular and Fabulous rooms cost a few bucks more, and come with

their own sun patio or private garden. Extreme WOW suites are in a different pay grade altogether, with a dining room for ten and an open-air Jacuzzi overlooking the Bosphorus. Drinking and dining are reasons to visit the W alone, not least as the hotel has one of the few alfresco terraces in the city – and a massive one at that. Indoors, Frederic's does formal elegance and Italian cuisine, while the W Lounge – where breakfast is also served – is a hip hangout with art books, Turkish tapas and nightly DJs. Minyon, also indoors, features one of Istanbul's hottest young chefs and an all-female kitchen line-up. W makes up for the classic Istanbul issue of no pool in the best possible way. Guests receive complimentary access to Su Ada, a funky floating pontoon pool just up the Bosphorus.

Style 8, Atmosphere 8, Location 7

....

eat...

If you hate history, monuments and sightseeing, have a deep-seated aversion to nightclubs and bars, aren't remotely interested in shopping and are allergic to all physical activities, you can still have a brilliant time in Istanbul by eating. In doing so you would be following in a great imperial tradition, for in the pursuit of gastronomic indulgence the Ottoman sultans led from the front, their vast personal kitchens, at their height, employing 1,300 staff to blend traditions, ingredients and flavours culled from all corners of the empire.

Sadly Ottoman chefs, strict adherents to the thesis that knowledge is power, never wrote anything down and the few restaurants that claim to purvey *saray* (palace) cuisine with its unusual combinations of sweet and savoury tastes, including Tuğra, Asitane and the elegant Feriye, make great bones of their historical detective work in piecing together recipes.

The basic, though delicious, Turkish diet has rather humbler origins. Its meatcentricity stretches back to the nomadic past when Turkic tribes took their larders with them in the form of assorted hoofed animals. The grilled meat tradition is upheld in countless *kebabçı* (kebab joints) and *ocakbaşı* (where the food will be grilled in front of you), most of which are excellent. Nor is the millennia-old culinary tradition static – the döner kebab was only invented in 1867, in Western Turkey. Nonetheless, a few famous and more pricey establishments vie for the reputation of making the best kebab in Istanbul (and by extension the world), prime among them: Beyti, Develi, Hacı Abdullah and Hamdi.

Then there is the *meyhane*, exponent of the Mediterranean tradition of *meze*. Here the tiny area of Asmalımescit, near the bottom of Istiklal Caddesi, offers some of the best, including Refik and Yakup 2. Bottles of *rakı* and a general hubbub accompany the myriad of dishes on offer, including fish, meat and loads of olive oil-doused veggies. More raucous, less genteel but immensely popular are the many *meyhaneler* that pack nearby Nevizade Sokak. Quite different, but equally authentic, is Çiya, an unpretentious but superb restaurant on the Asian side that produces masterpieces of Anatolian cooking.

The key to the quality of these traditional Turkish establishments is the freshness of the ingredients. This quality is unsurprisingly also prevalent in Istanbul's many fish restaurants, of which Kordon Balik, Doğa Balık and Bebek Balıkçı are the best. For the ultimate in freshness and personal choice, however, head to the fish market by Galata Bridge, pick your (possibly still wriggling) piscine date for the night and walk around the corner where a nice man in a hat will grill it for you.

Finally, there is the raft of über-stylish new restaurants that have opened over the last decade, offering international and fusion cuisine, which are magnets for Istanbul's brightly dressed-up young things (and their older, wealthier, sugar daddies). Changa, one of the first and still one of the best, is joined by Vogue, with its spectacular views, Zuma, Mimolett and Minyon. The standard of food is high in all these restaurants, and is generally more than matched by the visual delights on offer. On an equally innovative yet less expensive note are the city's hip *trattorias*, which offer Turko-Mediterranean cuisine to a more relaxed clientele. Many opened during Istanbul's Capital of Culture 2010 year including Karaköy Lokantası and Lokanta Maya in the newly-cool Karaköy docks area.

The price given is for three courses and half a bottle of wine per person.

What's on the menu?

Tuğra

our favourite restaurants...

Asitane
Çiya
Feriye
Kanaat Lokantasi
Kordon Balik
Lokanta Maya
Maya Lokantasi
Mimolett
Tuğra
Yakup 2

Beyti
Çiya
Kanaat Lokantasi
Mimolett
Tuğra

Beyti
Galata House
Kordon Balik
Seasons
Tuğra

Changa
Feriye
Karaköy fish market
Refik
Yakup 2

Asitane *(left)*
Kariye Hotel, Camii Sokak 18,
Edirnekapı
Tel: 00 90 212 635 7997
www.asitanerestaurant.com
Open: daily, 11am–midnight
Turkish (Ottoman) **100TL**

Next to the beautiful Church of Christ in Chora in the west of the Old City, Asitane is on the lower level of the Kariye Hotel. In a smartish, formal setting, the restaurant serves up classic Ottoman *saray* (palace) cuisine. However, Ottoman cooks prided themselves on never writing anything down. There is a famous anecdote told of the pastry chef of a visiting French royal who met his Turkish counterpart in the imperial kitchens and hoped to pick up a recipe or two. As they began talking

the Frenchman pulled out his measuring spoons, weight and scales and notebook, aiming for a certain precision of information exchange, whereupon the Turk seized them and threw them out of the nearest window in disgust, pointing out that cooking is an art dependent on the constant application of finely-tuned sensitivities and judgments, not a question of robotically following a set of instructions. Consequently, the chefs at Asitane, Feriye and Tuğra, the three Ottoman restaurants in this selection, spend as much time scouring historical accounts of imperial feasts as sourcing ingredients. On the menu at the time of writing, for example, is a recreation of dishes served up at the circumcision feast of one of Süleyman the Magnificent's sons, including almond soup and meats stewed with fruits and seasoned with cinnamon and honey. The starter selection includes minced meat-stuffed melon – a dish that dates from 1539 – and cinnamon liver patties – a palace creation from 1695.

Food 9, Service 8, Atmosphere 6

■ **Balıkcı Sabahattin**   *(right)*
Seyti Hasan Kuyu Sokak 50,
off Cankurtaran, Sultanahmet
Tel: 00 90 212 458 18 24
www.balikcisabahattin.com
Open: daily, noon–1am
Fish/Seafood   **110TL**

The best fish restaurant in the Old City is also one of the best in Greater Istanbul. It draws in customers from all over, who come to sit in its pretty outdoor terrace or its crumbling bourgeois mansion house. And before the brilliant seafood selection has got anywhere near your table they've been vetted by Balıkcı Sabahattin's proprietor, Mr. Sabahattin Cankurtaran, who is up at the crack of dawn trawling the fish markets to get his hands on the day's best catches. The restaurant featured in the New York Times a decade ago and for many, this listing was its downfall. Over the last few years, standards certainly haven't slipped but prices have risen and the waiters are more harried and are thus more likely to hurry a non-Turkish speaker through proceedings. But when faced with a *meze* platter of spiced fish balls, marinated sea bass and grilled calamari you're likely to forgive any misdemeanours and dive straight in. Train buffs should note that Istanbul's suburban rail line abuts the res-

taurant, and Orient Express trains used to pass along it until the 1970s. A handful of carriages bound for Belgrade and Bucharest still amble by each night.

Food 9, Service 5, Atmosphere 7

....

La Brise *(left)*
Asmalımescit 28, Tünel
Tel: 00 90 212 244 4846
www.cokcok.com.tr
Open: noon–midnight. Closed Mondays.
French **90TL**

Amidst the plethora of restaurants and cafes in Tünel, La Brise is the first up-market brasserie to open in the area. Launched in 2008 on the ground floor of a previously derelict late 19th-century townhouse, La Brise has helped to gentrify this busy street behind the Marmara Pera hotel. The interior is decked out with plush cherry wood furniture, leather-clad seating, Art Deco mirrors and white-clothed tables, a setting that aims for decadence of the most high-end order. Prices here are surprisingly in keeping with – if not more modest than – the neighbouring traditional *meze* restaurants, although the foreign wines are as pricey as anywhere. While French cuisine is the theme *du jour*, the menu is not so nationally strict, and it offers a range of salads, steaks and even pork. A fine combination of visual seduction and rigid table etiquette, La Brise is particularly well suited for an impressive business dinner or romantic night out, especially if a formal lay of cutlery is important for your guest/s.

Food 8, Service 7, Atmosphere 6

....

Bebek Balıkçı *(middle)*
Küçük Bebek, Cevdat
Paşa Caddesi 26, Bebek
Tel: 00 90 212 263 3447
www.bebekbalikci.net

Open: daily, noon–2am
Fish/Seafood 130TL

Several of Istanbul's top fish restaurants are located some way from either the Old City or Beyoğlu, so that the visitor who travels to them for lunch or dinner has the faint air of making a pilgrimage. If you do undertake the trek up to Bebek Balıkçı, nestling in the affluent locale of Bebek, any doubt as to whether the journey was worth it will be quickly smoothed away by the opening array of seaweed salad, preserved tuna (eaten with raw onion), stuffed mussels and caviar. The outdoor terrace, which almost hangs over the Bosphorus, will impress just as much, and last, but certainly not least, is the fish – super-fresh, as one would expect, and prepared with consummate skill. Book in advance.

Food 9, Service 7, Atmosphere 7

Beyti *(right)*
Orman Sokak 8, Florya
Tel: 00 90 212 663 2990
www.beyti.com
Open: 11.30am–11.30pm.
Closed Mondays
Turkish 120TL

Beyti Güler is a legend in his own lunchtime, probably the only living Turk to have a kebab named after him (the Beyti kebab, obviously – minced lamb with garlic and peppers served in filo pastry). His family opened their first restaurant in 1945, quickly gaining a reputation for serving a nicely done bit of meat. Beyti launched his current establishment in the 1970s and it is, in kebab terms, the Holy of Holies, a 3,000-square-metre palace of carnivorous pleasure with 11 dining rooms and five kitchens. Other places grow their own vegetables; Beyti rears its own lamb. It's not the substantial taxi-ride to reach the place (it's out near the

airport) that has charmed the world but the establishment's lovely tender chops, which you should make a point of trying. Beyti also does a nice line in faded politicians. Two of his most famous customers have been Richard Nixon and Jimmy Carter. An essential stop for enthusiastic meat-eaters (unless you're an aspiring US president).

Food 10, Service 8, Atmosphere 8

■ **Borsa** *(left)*
Istanbul Convention and Exhibition Centre (Lütfi Kırdar Kongere Merkezi), Darülbedai Caddesi 6, Harbiye
Tel: 00 90 212 232 4201
www.borsarestaurant.com
Open: daily, noon–3.30pm, 6.30pm–midnight.
Turkish **100TL**

Widely considered to be one of the best Turkish restaurants in town, this Borsa is a chic part of an old, family-run chain, which began 75 years ago. The location is a bit of a duffer, being the unappealing Istanbul Convention and Exhibition Centre in Harbiye, just north of Taksim Square. Nevertheless, Istanbul's well-heeled professionals flock in from the surrounding smart neighbourhoods and regularly fill out the restaurant's 500-person capacity, giving the place a convivial buzz. The service is super-slick and highly-attentive for such a large place and the food, too, is top-notch, with the usual Turkish menu of *meze* followed by a deliciously meaty selection of mains. The classic Turkish aubergine dish, *Imam bayıldı*, meaning 'the Imam fainted' (because it was so delicious rather than because of food poisoning), the oven-cooked lamb (*kuzu tandır*) and the grilled veal meatballs in pita (*dana köfte*) are perennial favourites. Reservations are essential.

Food 8, Service 8, Atmosphere 7

■ **Çok Çok** *(middle)*
Meşrutiyet Caddesi 51, Tepebaşı
Tel: 00 90 212 292 6496
www.cokcok.com.tr
Open: noon-midnight. Closed Mondays.
Asian **100TL**

Çok Çok sees itself as 'a bridge between cultures', but rather than hosting
the European fusion cuisine that such a
description would normally suggest, this
Thai restaurant is all about the meeting
of South East Asian and South West
Asian food, in terms of both culture
and design. The interior is designed to
blend the traditional and contemporary;
every table offers a gentle intimacy and
no detail has been overlooked from the
handcrafted paper lanterns to the opulent cushioned seating areas upstairs.
The only downside to Çok Çok's atmosphere are the views out arguably the
ugliest building in Istanbul. However,
when one takes into account the food –
which comprises Thai dishes made with

ingredients almost impossible to find in
Istanbul – all in all there is very little to
fault in this restaurant's refreshingly refined cuisine.

Food 8, Service 7, Atmosphere 6

■ **Changa** *(right)*
Sıraselviler Caddesi 87/1, Taksim
Tel: 00 90 212 251 7064
www.changa-istanbul.com
Open: daily, 6pm–1am (2am Fri/Sat).
Closed Sundays.
Fusion **120TL**

One of the pioneers (and still one
of the leaders) of Istanbul's super-
fashionable fusion cuisine revolution,
Changa is a destination station for Istanbul's smart set. Through the imposing entrance of a beautifully-detailed
Art Nouveau building in the large and
unlovely Sıraselviler Caddesi, you'll
find this slick, contemporary restau-

rant occupying several floors. Diners on the ground level will not only enjoy propping up the long, stylish bar, but also watching the kitchen staff at work in the basement below, thanks to the large Perspex porthole thoughtfully positioned into the floor. It provides a visceral reminder of the harsh reality of socio-economic relations (*Upstairs, Downstairs*, anyone?) but is eye-catching nonetheless. The menu, created by famed Kiwi fusion chef Peter Gordon, mixes South East Asian and Turkish tastes and ingredients. Grilled octopus with red miso and nori sauce, slow-cooked beef cheeks with goat's milk yoghurt and gremolata, and chilli-poached pears with buffalo milk mastic are just three of the inspiring choices.

Food 8, Service 7, Atmosphere 8

....

Çiya *(top)*
Güneşlibahçe Sokak 43, Kadiköy
Tel: 00 90 216 330 3190
www.ciya.com.tr
Open: daily, 11am–10pm
Turkish (Anatolian)   **50TL**

A restaurant worth crossing continents for. This fact won't immediately be apparent, as Çiya, only a few streets away from the ferry port in Kadiköy, is unassuming in appearance. But this culinary outpost has become one of the city's principal ports of call for serious foodies – although its keen prices make it equally popular with lunching local workers. In short, Çiya serves up award-winning Anatolian cooking with nuance and sophistication. The restaurant's assimilation of culinary traditions from various Turkish regions is evident in the

selection of unusual tasting stews, meat and vegetable dishes. Try eggplant and onion *bas kavurma* from Adana, chickpea and eggplant stems *bork* asi from Gaziantep, and beef-stuffed wild greens from distant Kastamonu. Desserts are equally novel, including creamy puddings with the odd surprising savoury ingredients such as roasted corn and grape molasses from Lake Van and a nutty pumpkin pudding from the Syrian borderland. Çiya may be alcohol-free but a medley of blackberry sherbet, cactus syrup or homemade lemonade are tailor-made to blend with the heartiest of Anatolian appetites. Note that there are in fact three Çiyas – two Çiya Kebapçıs, highly recommended meat joints with vast vegetable appetiser selections on the opposite side of the road – and Çiya Sofrası, the one listed here. All are superb.

Food 9, Service 8, Atmosphere 6

....

Develi *(bottom)*
Samatya Balık Pazarı,
Gümüşyüzük Sokak 7, Samatya
Tel: 00 90 212 529 0833
www.develikebap.com
Open: daily, noon–midnight
Turkish (Anatolian)   **100TL**

Since 1912, Develi has been delivering spicy kebabs and other traditional south-east Anatolian dishes to the city. Its excellent reputation has survived the decades intact and the original restaurant occupies a large, ornamental wooden building on the long costal road that stretches along the Sea of Marmara from the Old City towards the airport. The drive is worth it, an

opinion shared by the clientele that comes from miles around. Perennial favourites are the *çiğ köfte* (steak tartar-type meatballs) and the delicious *keme kebab* (cooked with apple and walnuts). Like its patrons' waistlines, Develi has expanded over recent years, and now includes restaurants in Kalamış, in Kadıköy's marina, Etiler and Ataşehir.

Food 8, Service 7, Atmosphere 7

Doğa Balık *(top)*
Hotel Villa Zurich, Akarsu Yokuşu Caddesi 46, Cihangir
Tel: 00 90 212 243 3656
www.dogabalik.com.tr
Open: daily, noon–2am
Fish/Seafood **120TL**

Another of Istanbul's top fish restaurants, Doğa Balık is found above the Hotel Villa Zurich in trendy central Cihangir, which locals describe as an odd location for a fish restaurant as it's 'in town' as opposed to being on the seashore, which is all of five minutes away. Happily, this means it's in easy reach if you're hanging around Beyoğlu. A mesmerising view across the water to Sultanahmet is merely a bonus. The real draw is the simply served but delicious *meze* and fish. A particular speciality is vegetarian meze that run to around 50 awesome dishes including a score of different steamed greens, seaweeds and herbs in olive oil (which makes Doğa Balık an excellent vegetarian option, too). As for the fish, try some grilled bonito, bream or bluefish with onions and herbs. Diners should be aware of an all too frequent gross up-selling, however – the waiter's description of a table-sized turbot may sound good but can make for a shock when you divvy up the bill later that night. This naughtiness aside, it's a sure-fire bet.

Food 9, Service 5, Atmosphere 7

Feriye *(bottom)*
Feriye Sarayı,
Çırağan Caddesi 40, Ortaköy
Tel: 00 90 212 227 2216
www.feriye.com
Open: daily, noon–3pm, 7pm–midnight
Turkish (Ottoman) **120TL**

The closest you can get, in restaurant terms, to the world of the late Ottoman elites is Feriye, set in a beautifully-restored and particularly grand old police station within palatial grounds that once belonged to the Çırağan Palace. Set up by celebrity chef Vedat Basaran, Feriye, like Asitane and nearby Tuğra, serves up *saray* (palace) cuisine, playing detective to unearth old Ottoman and even Byzantine techniques often applied with a contemporary twist. In the restaurant's own words, the menu serves an 'up-to-date synthesis of traditional Turkish and Ottoman cuisine'. The seasonal menu is dominated by whatever fresh ingredients are available, while signature dishes include air-dried beef wrapped in vine leaves and homemade *mantı* (ravioli) stuffed with pine nuts. For the best in succulent meat, try the milk-fed lamb served on charcoal-grilled aubergine purée with yoghurt and *perde pilav* with raisins. The waterside summer dining terrace on the banks of the Bosphorus is divine.

Food 9, Service 7, Atmosphere 9

Galata House *(left)*
Kulesi Sokak 61, Galata
Tel: 00 90 212 245 1861
Open: noon–midnight. Closed Mondays.
Georgian/Russian   **60TL**

When it comes to charming eccentricity, Galata House beats every other Istanbul restaurant hands-down. Run by the multi-skilled Nadire and Mete Göktug, architects with a strong sideline in cooking, it occupies an attractively-worn 18th-century building just off Galata Tower that used to the old British prison. There, under a special dispensation from the sultans, the British incarcerated their own errant subjects. In what is the certainly the most distinctive interior design scheme among the city's many restaurants, the Göktugs have wisely preserved those poor souls' doodled graffiti along with passages of peeling paint from the pe-

riod. Particularly notable are the naïve but powerful renderings of various wardens along with a selection of their attractively-shaped hats. The simple, homely furniture and decoration combined with the Göktugs' friendliness soon dispense any thoughts of imprisonment. Mete will sit down and have a chat while Nadire will rustle up the menu's Georgian, Russian and Tartar delicacies, all from her Crimean homeland. Then, if you're really lucky, she'll have a tinkle on the ivories, throwing wild Georgian songs into the mix. A fine selection of Caucasian wine completes the mix.

Food 7, Service 8, Atmosphere 8

Hamdi *(middle)*
Kalcin Sokak 17,
Tahmis Caddesi, Eminönü

Tel: 00 90 212 528 0390
www.hamdi.com.tr
Open: daily, 11.30am–midnight
Turkish (Anatolian)   **90TL**

Just on the south side of Galata Bridge and around the corner from the Egyptian Bazaar is Hamdi, one of Istanbul's premier purveyors of deluxe kebabs, almost on a par with the legendary Beyti. The principal reason for the quality is the consistent and expert attention of Mr. Hamdi, who, along with his bristling moustache, keeps a dictatorial eye on all proceedings. The dishes from southeast Anatolia (the original home of the kebab) include the lovely *fıstık* kebab, made with pistachio nuts, the *erikli* kebab, with plums, and the *testi* kebab, a sealed clay pot in which lamb and vegetables simmer to a rare succulence. In summer you'll sit up on the rooftop terrace with its gorgeous views across

the Golden Horn toward the Galata Tower. The delicious food engenders a passionate and loyal following among discerning carnivores across the city, although long-term patrons have been joined by Istanbul's tourist hordes (including many tour groups) so curt service in English is sadly now the norm.

Food 8, Service 5, Atmosphere 7

Hacı Abdullah   *(right)*
Atıf Yılmaz Caddesi 9,
off İstiklal Caddesi, Beyoğlu
Tel: 00 90 212 293 8561
www.haciabdullah.com.tr
Open: daily, 11am–10.30pm
Turkish (Ottoman)   **60TL**

Open for over 120 years, Hacı Abdullah lays claim as the city's oldest restaurant. It was serving up Turkish and

Ottoman delicacies way back when. Hacı Abdullah doesn't wear its age on its sleeve, however. Its large, spacious interior has a contemporary but warm feel, thanks to the wall-to-ceiling wood and the rows upon rows of huge jars of brightly-coloured, pickled vegetables. If you go, sit in the back room, which is the nicest. The food – *meze*, soups, stews and kebabs – and service is universally good, and the meaty mains – which include slow-roasted lamb shank and several traditional beef stews – take some beating. The place is easily accessible, too, so if you're in town just for a few days and looking for an easy-to-find, quality Turkish restaurant, Hacı Abdullah is an excellent choice. No alcohol is served and the place closes earlier than many of its rivals, so lunch could be the best option here.

Food 8, Service 7, Atmosphere 8

....

Kanaat Lokantası *(top)*
Selmanipak Caddesi 9, Üsküdar
Tel: 00 90 216 341 5444
www.kanaatlokantasi.com.tr
Open: daily, noon–10pm
Turkish **50TL**

Üsküdar's top table has consistently offered some of city's finest food since 1933. The classic venue is not a place to linger, however. Notoriously uncomfy upright chairs and a lack of alcohol – Kanaat lies in Istanbul's most pious quarter – make dining functional if exceptionally flavourful. The unworldly waiters hover impatiently, too, and call out 'soup' or 'lamb' in a kind yet ultimately unhelpful attempt to assist your order. But there's no need to be hurried.

A vast open buffet runs the whole side of the room with around 40 appetisers displayed behind the glass. Grab your waiter and point at dishes like Circassian chicken with walnut sauce, or *cacık*, a raita-style garlic and cucumber yoghurt. The hot mains counter is manned by four smiley chefs in tall white hats, ready to carve, grill and plonk down your order. Try *hindi dolma*, a crispy stuffed turkey dish, or *parmak* kebab, a succulent lamb casserole infused with aubergine. Desserts are of an artery-clogging intensity. Classics include *incir tatlısı* – an unctuous creamy fig pudding – and *tavuk göğsü* – a sweet chicken breast dish that's far nicer than it sounds.

Food 9, Service 7, Atmosphere 7

....

Karaköy Fish *(bottom)*
Market Restaurants
Karaköy Balıkçı Sokak
Open: daily, noon–midnight
Fish/Seafood **40TL**

Kumkapı used to be the best place to go if you wanted nice fresh fish, simply prepared. Nowadays, you might try heading for the fish market on the Beyoğlu side of Galata Bridge, buying a fish of your choice and walking around the corner where, in a couple of crotchety buildings on the edge of a rare patch of grass sprinkled with a couple of tables, you can find men with grills who'll cook up your catch for you. Of course, they have stock of their own, so you don't actually have to buy the fish yourself and run the embarrassing risk of turning up with a dud that their expert eye would have spotted a nautical mile off. Two favourite hole-in-the-wall establishments – complete with laminated A4 menus – are Balikche and Akın Balık. The scene is especially nice at night, when you can sit at candlelit tables among the trees on the shores of the Golden Horn – one of the most bucolic, most authentic and least expensive dining experiences in the city.

Food 8, Service 7, Atmosphere 9

Karaköy Lokantası *(top)*
Kemankes Caddessi, Karaköy
Tel: 00 90 212 292 4455
www.karakoylokantasi.com
Open: midday–4pm, 6pm–
midnight. Closed Sundays.
Fish/Seafood **90TL**

The rapidly regenerating Karaköy docks area is the venue for this chic seafood trattoria, which wouldn't look out of place in Milan. From start to finish this establishment is smart, personable and smacks of good taste. Inside the Italian influence carries forth with aqua-blue *tomette* floor tiles and an inspired seating arrangement of quiet dining booths, romantic tables for two and a handful of 'who's-the-daddy' showpiece banquettes. There's a relaxed upstairs and a pleasantly rough-around-the-edges outdoor terrace, too. But it's the food that really pulls in the punters (well-dressed regulars that they are). Grilled octopus (to-die-for) and fish steaks grace the main menu along with a few meaty options including marinated fried liver and flame-seared lamb chops. A solid *rakı* selection – connoisseurs can try Altınbaş or Cilingir, classic imbibers Efe or Tekirdağ – is on offer to wash down a memorable meal.

Food 8, Service 7, Atmosphere 7

Kordon Balik *(middle)*
Kuleli Caddesi 51, Çengelköy
Tel: 00 90 216 321 0473
www.kordonbalik.com
Open: daily, 7pm–midnight
Fish/Seafood **150TL**

Kordon is an exquisite treat in more ways than one. Hugging the Bosphorus in the oh-so-pretty village of Çengelköy, it welcomes guests arriving by water taxi to its private jetty while the valet out front parks more regular motorised transport. Architecturally it's pretty special, too, occupying part of a late Ottoman waterside warehouse with high ceilings and plate glass windows looking out to sea (the sublime Sumahan Hotel occupies the rest of the building right next door). But what Kordon's classy customers come for is the fisherman-fresh seafood that hails from the Black Sea in winter (turbot, sole and flounder) and from more local waters in summer (swordfish, grouper and bream). *Meze* include salted tuna and tiny, spicy stuffed bell peppers, plus local Çengelköy cucumbers – which are said to be the world's tastiest.

Food 9, Service 9, Atmosphere 7

Kumkapı Meyhanes *(bottom)*
Kumkapı
Open: most are open daily, noon–2am
Fish/Seafood **65TL**

An old Greek and Armenian fishing district on the Sea of Marmara, Kumkapı is a brief taxi ride from the centre of the Old City. For a while it was one of the best places in town for

fish fans. Simplicity was a virtue, with a clutch of *meyhaneler* that opened up around a lovely square serving fresh fish in a lively environment. When it's warm, and all the seating is outside, the place still has a good buzz about it, but popularity with tourists has brought a certain naffness, and a reputation for its restaurateurs as a little dishonest – short-changing customers, bringing you dishes you didn't order, and so on. However, many of the establishments still serve plenty of tasty fish, and if you're in the area and hungry it remains a good bet. Restaurants like Okyanus and Patara, off the main square, are recommended, where the food is a straightforward fish *meze* and can be very good.

Food 6, Service 5, Atmosphere 7

Lokanta Maya *(left)*
Kemankeş Caddesi 35, Karaköy
Tel: 00 90 212 251 1042
www.lokantamaya.com

Open: noon–11pm. Closed Sunday
Modern Turkish **70TL**

Didem Şenol's path to superstar chefdom has been a unique one. After learning her trade in the kitchens of New York City, she spent five years in a small village on Turkey's blissfully peaceful Aegean coast sourcing regional recipes and learning about localised ingredients. Her resulting cookbook, *Aegean Flavours*, is a must in every chic Istanbul home, and her blog and newspaper recipe column are local foodie favourites. She hit the jackpot by opening this restaurant in the trendy Karaköy docks area in 2010 – an informal, elegant establishment that could be in NYC if the decibel levels were higher – and her ever-changing seasonal menu has been bringing in the hungry hordes. Dishes are reassuringly uncomplicated: this is not a restaurant that hides its inadequacy under a smokescreen of fussy emulsions and fusion-esque potions. This is especially true with the six or

seven appetisers. A regular is the sea bass carpaccio dotted with Didem's father's olive oil – squished against the roof of the mouth, it becomes a nutty sweet purée. These starters tee up the wow-factor mains, where Didem balances flavours as diverse as crunchy caramelised sea bass with a seasonal fruit – be it apricot, orange or fig – to draw out the fish's sweetness. Yummy.

Food 9, Service 8, Atmosphere 8

Mia Mensa *(middle)*
Muallim Naci Caddesi 64,
Kuruçeşme
Tel: 00 90 212 263 4214
www.miamensa.com
Open: daily, noon–2am
Italian   **120TL**

During the summer months chic Mia Mensa boasts a lovely location, sharing a waterside terrace with Aşşk Café on the nightlife strip of Kuruçeşme. The cuisine is Italian, excellently prepared

with the freshest ingredients accompanied by a decent wine list and solid service. It's an atmospheric spot for lunch, when the profusion of blue parasols offer shade while the Bosphorus basks in the sunshine. But the place is particularly enchanting at night, especially on a clear evening, when you can watch the tankers sailing by en-route to Odessa and Constanta as you enjoy your antipasti. During winter, meals are served in the cosy confines of a wooden villa, which is also a popular venue for mid-afternoon mojitos and snacks.

Food 7, Service 7, Atmosphere 8

Mimolett *(right)*
Sıraselviler Caddesi 55, Cihangir
Tel: 00 90 212 245 9858
www.mimolett.com.tr
Open: 7pm–midnight. Closed Sunday
Mediterranean   **150TL**

Mimolett is a must for foodies, not least because of the calibre of its

30-something head chef Murat Bozok. His first big posting was working in one of French restaurant ace Pierre Gagnaire's kitchens in Paris, with further stints alongside Gordon Ramsay and Angela Hartnett at London's Connaught. After a stretch back in Paris with Joël Robuchon – as you do – Bozok is gunning for Michelin glory in the 'bul and has a refined southern French, Italian and Turkish repertoire to aid him on his path to gastro-greatness. Osso buco with foie gras and white bean *ourée* sits near wild seabass with nettle *velouté* on the main menu, while a degustation tasting carte takes taste to another level. Like many hip locales in the area, minimally elegant décor, a private dining room, vast outdoor terrace overlooking the Bosphorus and a sexy bar area come with the package.

Food 10, Service 9, Atmosphere 8

Minyon W Istanbul *(top)*
Suleyman Seba Caddesi 22,
Akaretler, Beşiktaş
Tel: 00 90 212 381 2121
www.wminyon.com
Open: daily, noon–11pm (2am Fri/Sat)
Eclectic **120TL**

W Hotel's super-chic dining option hosts more mirrors, models and brushed aluminium tables than your average Armani outlet. By day this hip hangout is the Akaretler shopping area's lunch spot *du jour.* The big Bose speakers at ground level hint at proceedings later in the evening when nighttime diners chomp to the throb of DJ sets and live acts – the tagline

is 'Hip Food, Hip Music' – and you'll either love it or hate it. The Turko-Japanese menu is as showy as it is expansive, although tasting platters give you a chance to nibble all of head chef Emre Çapa's creations. Lemongrass scallops and edamame salmon salad grace the starter menu, followed by Asian fish fillets and cracking pizzas on the more Turkish-heavy main selection.

Food 7, Service 7, Atmosphere 8

Nevizade Sokak *(bottom)*
off Çicek Pasajı,
off İstiklal Caddesi, Beyoğlu
Open: daily, noon–midnight or 2am
Turkish **70TL**

Not a single restaurant but a narrow street that runs off the covered fish market, just around the corner from Çicek Pasajı – the latter is a lovely 19th-century passageway full of attractive-looking restaurants (in addition to pesky touts trying to lure passing tourists in). Here, the 20 or so more down-to-earth eateries on Nevizade Sokak pull in tourists, too, but the generous helping of locals who fill the tables on both sides of the street helps to dilute the touts. When the place gets going there's a great energy, full of noise and action: waiters scurry back and forth with huge trays of *meze* while *fasıl* musicians ply their trade. The restaurants are invariably good, with slight variations between them being a bias towards dishes from one region or another, or a particular reputation for good live music. Take your time strolling by and pick one that takes your fancy. A good place to head to on your first night in the city, just to

make sure you get into the swing of things quickly.

Food 7, Service 6, Atmosphere 8

....

■ **Niş**   *(top)*
■ *Abdi İpekçi Caddesi 40/C,*
Nişantaşı
Tel: 00 90 212 296 9555
www.nisistanbul.com
Open: daily, noon–midnight
Turkish/European   **110TL**

At the heart of the chicville that is Ni şantaşı is Niş, a restaurant/bar where locals often seek sustenance to fuel another few hours of vital shopping. The atmosphere's buzzy and energetic, and the clientele suitably elegant. The menu never stands still but is always rich and varied, with a mixture of Turkish and European tastes, dishes and options for those calorie-controlled fashionistas searching for a special salad as well as hungry visitors looking for a rump steak burger or a smoked salmon fettuccine. Live jazz and cocktails draw people to the upstairs bar, as does the happy hour on Saturdays.

Food 6, Service 7, Atmosphere 8

....

■ **Pandeli**   *(left)*
■ *Mısır Çarşısı 1, Eminönü*
Tel: 00 90 212 527 3909
www.pandeli.com.tr
Open: noon–4pm. Closed Sundays.
Turkish   **100TL**

An Istanbul classic that draws on over a century of culinary experience, Pandeli is a haven of calm situated above the riotous bustle of the Egyptian Bazaar, which is something of a dining black hole. From the ancient doorway through which you have to pass, to the terrific, decorative, blue and turquoise tiles, Pandeli has one of the most atmospheric and quintessentially Old Stamboul settings one can imagine, including a few tiny windows that offer a peek out onto the nearby Galata Bridge. As a result of its décor and location, Pandeli attracts droves of tourists and the management and staff takes full advantage. Reports suggest that the staff can be pushy for tips, though we haven't found this on our visits. Dishes are all Turkish classics from bean soup to tandoori lamb. None of the items really live up to the restaurant's rarified surroundings but the location and the feeling of the place are superb, so other deficiencies are well worth ignoring. Note that Pandeli serves lunch only.

Food 7, Service 5, Atmosphere 8

....

■ **Refik**   *(right)*
■ *Sofyalı Sokak 7–12,*
Asmalımescit, Tünel
Tel: 00 90 212 243 2834
www.refikrestaurant.com
Open: noon–3pm, 6pm–midnight.
Closed Saturday lunch and Sundays.
Turkish   **100TL**

Refik opened in 1954 and is owned by Refik Arslan. It is one of the most famous *meyhaneler* in town (and you should visit at least one while in Istanbul), offering the classic combination of *meze* and *rakı*. It has long attracted a loyal following among Istanbul's political intellectuals and is apparently full of lefties, the kind of people who know how to talk. Unfortunately, ignorance of Turkish may leave you oblivious to their incisive comments on dialectic materialism and the relationship between Kemalism and Socialism. Nevertheless, when you dine here you're dropping in on a real local scene, especially in winter, when you're confined to the simple but smart interior, decorated with myriad photos, and everything feels intimate and convivial. In summer, Refik's tables join the general, lively eating free-for-all that has now colonised the entirety of Sofyalı Sokak, a state of affairs for which Refik's popularity has been largely responsible. If you want to try the *meze* dishes in Refik (or any of its surrounding restaurants) just select them by pointing at them in glass-fronted fridges. So at least the language barrier won't get in the way of your stomach.

Food 7, Service 5, Atmosphere 8

Seasons Restaurant *(top)*
Four Seasons Hotel,
Tevfikhane Sokak 1, Sultanahmet
Tel: 00 90 212 402 3000
Open: daily, noon–3pm, 7–11pm
European **175TL**

One of the finest European restaurants in Istanbul belongs to the Four Seasons in Sultanahmet, an establishment that recently won the rather blandly titled but no doubt prestigious 'best hotel restaurant in Turkey' award. The setting is an elegant conservatory and beautiful courtyard, which errs on the tasteful side of opulence. The menu changes every season, adapting to the best of what's locally available, but dishes are generally adorned with touches of French finery, Italian classicism and the odd nod to the Far East. Regulars also include dishes such as grilled sea bass, perfectly-seared, while short-term, special regional menus – such as a recent collection of dishes from Turkey's Hatay province – are exceptional. The Sunday brunch is also legendary and should be experienced, if only for a peek at the city's high society. Pricey by Istanbul standards, it's a lavish affair that should set you up for a great siesta. Smart threads and a reservation are a must.

Food 8, Service 9, Atmosphere 7

Sunset Grill & Bar *(bottom)*
Yol Sokak 1, off Adnan
Saygun Caddesi, Ulus Parkı, Ulus
Tel: 00 90 212 287 0357
www.sunsetgrillbar.com
Open: daily, noon–3pm, 7pm–2am
Eclectic **150TL**

A touch of California on the Bosphorus, Sunset has been open for more than a decade. The fact that it's still popular with the smart crowd and winning awards confirms its enduring quality. Set in the arboreal surrounding of Ulus Park, on a hill overlooking the Bosphorus, it has a stunning location (though it's a fair taxi ride from wherever you're likely to be), which it makes great use of with its lovely terrace, replete with contemporary, wave-shaped awnings. The food hails from three continents (Europe, Asia and America, melding towards a general fusion), seasoned

with the contents of the restaurant's own herb garden. The sushi is among best in the city, too, while the Turkish menu changes daily depending on what fantastic ingredients the chefs can get their hands on. Add one of Turkey's best wine cellars and you've got a fine, cool restaurant – an excellent dinner destination, from where you'll enjoy the myriad twinkling lights adorning the Bosphorus shores. Which, if you squint hard and have drunk a bit, almost look like stars.

Food 8, Service 7, Atmosphere 8

....

 Tokyo *(right)*
Meşelik Sokak 24,
off İstiklal Caddesi, Beyoğlu
Tel: 00 90 212 293 5858
Open: daily, noon–11pm
Japanese/Sushi   **90TL**

The latest sushi bar to open in town is assuredly one of the best. Located a California roll's throw from Taksim Square, Tokyo serves a spellbindingly large array of sushi made at the bar as you watch, as well as a selection of meat, noodle and rice dishes. Patrons dining solo or in pairs can choose to watch the world go by through the front glass façade, or sit at the bar and study the skills of the sushi master. Upstairs, a flexible floor-seated space can be split by sliding screens into a series of private bamboo-panelled rooms for groups of up to eight. If the party is even larger the whole space can be taken over by one sitting. If none of these spaces seem to suit then Tokyo also offers a free delivery service to your hotel door.

Food 8, Service 6, Atmosphere 6

....

Tuğra *(top)*
Çırağan Caddesi 32, Beşiktaş
Tel: 00 90 212 326 4646
www.kempinski.com
Open: daily, 7pm–midnight
Turkish (Ottoman)   **200TL**

Istanbul's doyen of fine-dining, Tuğra, is the city's top table by some distance. It's prim and elegant, too: ties are considered a show of class, trying to pour your own wine most certainly isn't. Cuisine under the tutelage of head chef Uğur Alparslan is classic Ottoman with many of the sumptuous, unctuous and fruity delicacies drawn from centuries-old palace cookbooks. The full-fat option at Tuğra is the multi-course tasting menu, best washed down with reds from Cappadocia and Bozcaada although several vintages of Chateau Lafite lie in state by the *salumeria* (yep, pork is served) and cheese counter. Main dishes arrive under a salver shaped like a Sultan's hat – a jolly novelty that offsets the strict formality somewhat. As you might expect from the showpiece restaurant at Istanbul's finest hotel – the Çırağan Palace – the views over the Bosphorus are priceless.

Food 10, Service 9, Atmosphere 7

....

Ulus 29 *(left)*
Kireçhane Sokak 1, Adnan
Saygun Caddesi, Ulus Parkı, Ulus
Tel: 00 90 212 358 2929
www.group-29.com

Open: daily, noon–4pm, 7pm–midnight
Turkish/Mediterranean   200TL

Located just above the swish Sunset Grill on the same hill is the similarly glamorous Ulus 29, with (again) fantastic views of the Bosphorus enjoyed from a lovely semi-circular terrace. Owned by lifestyle entrepreneur Metin Fadıllıoğlu and designed by his architect wife Zeynep, the restaurant is smartly decorated and perennially popular. The '29' bit of the name refers to the 29 classic dishes on the menu – Turkish and around the Eastern Med – all excellently prepared, if reassuringly expensive. Alternatively, you can have a spot of sushi, which seems oddly popular on this particular hill in Ulus (taking advantage, perhaps, of a secret local source of sushi chefs). The bar is notable, serving a good range of cocktails, making Ulus

29 all-in-all a great place to snack, imbibe and take in the view.

Food 7, Service 7, Atmosphere 8

Vogue   *(left)*
*Spor Caddesi 92, BJK Plaza
A Blok 13, Akaretler, Beşiktaş
Tel: 00 90 212 227 2545
Open: daily, 10.30am–3pm, 7pm–2am*
International   140TL

Arriving in the courtyard between a rash of anonymous office blocks is an unpromising start to this dining experience. But an assorted array of greeters, door-openers and ushers will quickly whisk you into a lift, which soon deposits you on the building's top floor and in another world. Better still is the amazing view. The food is a fine international mix of excellent sushi, top-drawer salads,

American-sized steaks and South-East Asian sides – all particularly accomplished. Sociologically speaking, Vogue has been a middle-class-and-made-it hangout for nearly a decade; so well-dressed – and well-heeled – families make up the midweek mainstay, with younger fashionistas at the weekend. The wine list is particularly extensive, as is the cigar selection: if you want to puff on a fat one, this is definitely the place. Sunday brunch here is also popular and highly recommended. We'll mention it again, that view really is to-die-for.

Food 7, Service 8, Atmosphere 7

Yakup 2 *(right)*
Asmalımescit Caddesi 35–37,
Tünel
Tel: 00 90 212 249 2925
www.yakuprestaurant.com

Open: daily, noon–2am
Fish/Seafood   100TL

Misty-eyed Beyolu old-timers will tell you that in days gone by a meyhane like Yakup 2 used to be so cheap that no one would bother cooking at home or buying the groceries, choosing to dine out at places like this most evenings. Now that Asmalımescit, once a haunt of pimps, ladies (and trannies) of the night and assorted bohemian types, has been hauled up a notch or two, everything's got a little more refined and foreigners have started dropping in, messing up the local ambience (but lengthening till receipts). Surviving local bohos still frequent the place, using the excuse of eating prodigious quantities of the excellent *meze* for drinking even more impressive quantities of rakı. The seafood-heavy mix of grilled, salt-baked and marinated fish puts the vast majority of Istanbul's newer, cooler locales to shame. The boisterous background noise and vast selections of food make it particularly amenable to groups, too, provided they book ahead.

Food 8, Service 7, Atmosphere 9

Zuma *(right)*
Salhane Sokak 7, Ortaköy
Tel: 00 90 212 236 2296
Open: daily, noon–1am
Japanese **180TL**

If food was everything then Zuma would be one of Istanbul's greats. The upscale Japanese restaurant chain works with such élan in London, Hong Kong and Miami and tastes just as good in Ortaköy. Like Tokyo, Turkish ingredients are top class if you're willing to pay for them, so truly yummy octopus, sea bass, lobster and crab are blended into spider rolls, seared beef *tataki*, salt-grilled bream and *isa ebi* chilli lobster. Décor is fun, too, and guests may play musical chairs around the sushi counter, the Robata grill, the dining room and the gorgeous summer terrace on the Bosphorus shores. Even hedonists might bulk at Zuma's price structure, however. It's bloody expensive and many squillionaires still regard value as a sensible commodity. Staff and punters alike can be a shade too cool for school, too: the latter forgivable, the former not so. But close your eyes/ears and gulp down a spicy tuna roll, and all can be quickly forgiven.

Food 9, Service 6, Atmosphere 7

drink

Long before they were Muslims, the Turks were drinkers. Old habits die hard, or, in this particular case, not at all. Instead they flourished and grew, helped along by the Ottomans' imaginatively liberal interpretation of religious strictures that have had a rather more sobering effect in many lands further east. Indeed, the hobby of extreme and sustained drinking was given the imperial imprimatur by a catalogue of inebriated sultans, such as Mahmut II, who managed to die of alcohol poisoning in 1839, and the aptly named Selim the Sot, who slipped and cracked his head on a soapy *hamam* floor after downing an entire bottle of Cypriot wine in 1574.

However, the habit wasn't adopted by the more God-fearing masses and consequently Turkey is not the land of one-thousand-and-one drinks, but three: *rakı*, beer and wine. *Rakı*, the national drink, is made from fermented grapes infused with aniseed and is similar to French *pastis*. Drunk with water or ice (only barbarians take it neat) it is the essential companion to *meze*. Efes is the refreshing, and suspiciously ubiquitous, leading Turkish beer (its marketing manager is clearly a dangerous megalomaniac – on many streets every shop hoarding and canopy is dedicated to Efes). Turkish wine has come on leaps and bounds in the last decade and is now winning awards in blind tastings against French Bordeaux. Large producers include Doluca (which owns the Kav and Villa Doluca vineyards) and Kavaklidere (which owns the lovely Yakut and lesser Angora, Sade and Dikmem brands). Truly excellent bottles you may wish to hunt down include Doluca's Sarafin Chardonnay and boutique producer Likya's Merlot-Syrah blend. New wine store-cum-bar Sensus near the Galata Tower allows you to sample wines from nearly every single producer in the country and is a great place to start. Imported spirits pay a hefty surcharge that has sadly stunted the growth of a cocktail culture, although this is rapidly changing in the hip bars around Tünel and Beyoğlu.

When it comes to drinking venues, however, Istanbul has an abundance of choice, including some of the most spectacular bars imaginable thanks to the city's wealth of outstanding views and vistas. Geographically, they are concentrated in Beyoğlu and in hotspots along the European Bosphorus shore such as Ortaköy and Kuruçe şme, with few notable options on the Asian side including Hush (which opened in 2010) and a new branch of 360° (which opened in 2011). It's also worth pointing out that many of the places separated here into the Drink, Eat, Party and Snack sections are in fact places where you can do all four (perhaps even all at once).

Around sunset on a summer's day there are few places better than sleekly modern Nu Teras, located on the seventh floor of a block in Pera, perfectly aligned as it is with the setting sun. Stunning panoramic views are also the raison d'être for 5-Kat, Leb-i-Derya and Vogue (see Eat), all crisply contemporary and popular with Istanbul's fashionable crowd.

Leb-i-Derya

Bars such as Badehane, in Asmalımescit, offer a simpler and more raucous atmosphere, while a string of 20-or so chicer bars line the surrounding streets – a fine place to eat, drink and be merry if ever there was. Meanwhile, the many indistinguishable Galata Bridge bars, though tacky in parts, present beautiful views of the Bosphorus if you're looking in the right direction (away from the bridge), especially at dusk.

For a contrast with all of the above and a hint of Old Stamboul try the elegant K.V., with its tasteful mix of the Viennese and Parisian styles that once gave Pera its dash, or the wonderfully eccentric bar at the fading Büyük Londra Hotel, which combines the varied charms of a caged parrot, Victorian décor, Ottoman chandeliers and slightly incompetent (but bow-tied) staff.

In Sultanahmet the Yesil Ev Garden is a rare, leafy oasis and the perfect place to recuperate after sightseeing. Indeed, the city garden bar has become a new and welcome trend during Istanbul's sub-tropical summers, and Ceyazir and Limonlu Bahçe are great places to sup and recline.

360° *(top)*
Istiklal Caddesi Mısır Apartmanı,
7th & 8th floors, Beyoğlu
Tel: 00 90 212 251 1042
www.360istanbul.com
Open: daily, 7pm–3am

Set up by people who clearly felt that Istanbul didn't quite have enough places with fantastic views, 360° occupies a purpose-built floor above a lovely, ornate period building slap-bang in the middle of Istiklal Caddesi. A club/bar/restaurant hybrid, it was once a hangout for the city's super-smart, trendy and glamorous set, who have now been replaced by a more middle-manager, touristy and showy set, but it's still good fun. The view, however, is pretty much timeless and envelopes two continents and several million people making you feel, ahem, on top of the world. There's one caveat, however. Staff members believe that working in a bar – even a cool one like this – gives them the right to sulk and pout their way through an evening service. Not so clever. A sister branch opened in a rooftop spot in Caferağa Mahallesi in Kadiköy in summer 2011.

5 Kat *(middle)*
Soğancı Sokak 7, Taksim
Tel: 00 90 212 293 3774
www.5kat.com
Open: daily, 10am–2am

Owned and run by Turkish actress Yasemin Alkaya, star of independent Turkish movies such as *Woman Smelling a Candle* and *Woman Without a Roof* (the titles lose something in the translation), the fifth-floor bar ('kat' meaning storey) is decked out with heavy, plush furniture and velvet drapes, all in dark, seductive colours, making it a good, if extremely camp, location for a winter's drink (or bite to eat). In summer – when heavy velvet becomes a little too outré even for 5 Kat regulars (assorted creative types) – the action moves upstairs to the lovely roof terrace, with, needless to say, excellent views of the surrounding city. Even in the sunshine, though, touches of kitsch survive, with a string of those brightly-coloured, swirly, plastic things that you can get in hippy-dippy shops decorating the bar. It's worth hunting down this slightly out-of-the way street off Sıraselviler Caddesi.

Badehane *(bottom)*
General Yazgan Sokak 5, Tünel
Tel: 00 90 212 249 0550
Open: daily, 9am–2am

This small, single room just off Sofayalı Sokak is one of the earliest colonisers of the once rough 'n' ready Asmalımescit bar zone and is still one of the best. Originally a haunt of an unwashed collection of liberals and poets, it's a shade more 21st-century now and attracts a nice, happy crowd, mainly in their 20s. Patrons still fall into spontaneous and raucous dancing, however, and backgammon tables remain stacked up on the bar counter. In winter a coal-fired brazier heats up the interior and the atmosphere becomes bookish, romantic and London pub once again. And since Badehane is located in the heart of lively Asmalımescit, you can have plenty of other picks to head to afterwards.

Bebek Hotel *(top)*
Cevdet Pafla Caddesi 34, Bebek
Tel: 00 90 212 358 2000
www.bebekhotel.com.tr
Open: daily, noon–1am

If you make it all the way up the Bosphorus to Bebek, make sure you stop for a coffee or a drink at the Bebek Hotel's wonderful bar, located on a veranda that hovers over the edge of the Bosphorus. The surrounding waterside houses and myriad moored yachts make for an idyllic scene, especially on a sunny spring or summer's day. The last word in Istanbullu elegance, the bar has been attracting the glamorous and well-heeled older set from the exclusive suburbs of north Istanbul for decades. While you're in Bebek don't forget to go and get some of the world's best marzipan from Bebek Badem Ezmecsi, just down the road.

....

Büyük Londra Hotel *(middle)*
Meşrutiyet Caddesi 53, Tepebaşı
Tel: 00 90 212 245 0670
www.londrahotel.net
Open: daily, 24 hours

For an antidote to the slick modernity of Istanbul's flock of fashionable new bars, head to the wonderfully eccentric bar of the Büyük Londra Hotel, in which a superannuated parrot is only one of the many aesthetic attractions, the other being the wonderfully OTT Victorian-period interior design and the curios dotted around. The place is likely to be fairly empty, but the staff is commendably relaxed and unlikely to mind if you started an enormous party of your own. The other major benefit of the Büyük Londra's bar is its promise of 24-hour drinking, though if you do stay for the full 24 hours it would only be polite if you were to book a room. The Londra is also the meeting place of Istanbul's large foreign correspondent contingent, which gathers here once a month to boast about recent scars gained in Herat, Gaza and Benghazi.

....

Ceyazir *(bottom)*
Hayrire Caddesi 12, Beyoğlu
Tel: 00 90 212 245 9980
www.cezayir-istanbul.com
Open: daily, 9am–2am

Ceyazir is the preserve of off-duty architects, creatives and various other aesthetes, and it's not hard to fathom why. Occupying almost every floor of a 1901 bourgeois mansion – which started life as the local Italian school – it surrounds the intelligent drinker with fine lines, lots of light and loads of good taste. The Nordic-style long bar is incongruous but remains its many residents favourite drinking place: a bare wood plinth lined with stools, staffed by an acquiescent barman and a DJ with a penchant for Jimmy Cliff. In the lounge area a dozen comfortably knackered armchairs sit on period tiles – sit in one of these and you'll never rise again. A fine if pricey contemporary Turkish restaurant serves mains in a delightful salon and dishes up yummy snacks throughout the building, including in the shady summer garden.

....

 **Galata Bridge Bars** *(left)*
Galata Bridge
Open: varies, but generally close around 2am.

The Galata Bridge is now in its fifth solid incarnation since 1845 and the current one, which dates from 1994, is hardly the prettiest. It does have one redeeming feature: rows of bars and restaurants along either side of its mezzanine level. Many are loud and tacky, others are naffly hip and favoured by out-of-town Turks keen to look cool, while some are the disco haunts of local geezers after hours.

However, all are fun for a pint by day, while at dusk they're great places to watch the sun set on the Golden Horn, which runs beneath the crossing. Later, if you want to keep up the rough 'n' ready tone for the evening, you can stroll to the small cooking establishments behind Galata's fish market and get yourself some fresh, grilled fish.

Gizli Bahçe *(top-right)*
Nevizade Sokak 5, Beyoğlu
Tel: 00 90 212 249 2192
Open: daily, noon–2am

It's called Gizli Bahçe, 'secret garden', for a reason. Without any sign at its entrance aside from a scrawled number 27 (plus an official '5' in red) it's difficult to find. In winter when the streets are empty you wouldn't know a bar was there at all, while in summer it's hard to differentiate Gizli Bahçe's crowd from the general melee on Nevizarde Sokak. Inside one finds a young (sometimes quite studenty), trendy (and trying-a-little-too-hard-to-be-trendy) crowd, nursing beers, posing and (probably) pontificating about popular culture. Two eclectic terraces overlook a backyard car park and peek into a few locals-only *meyhanes*, while the carefully-chosen, non-matching bits of scruffy furniture cement the youthful, creative atmosphere. Good fun for a cheap pint of local Efes lager.

....

Hush *(bottom-right)*
Miralay Nazım Sokak 20, Kadıköy
Tel: 00 90 216 450 43 63
hushistanbul.blogspot.com
Open: daily, 11am–1am (3am Fri/Sat)

As a sign of the times, Hush is another establishment that moved lock, stock from busy Taksim to the classy

but once crumbling seaside suburb of Kadiköy in 2010, where there's enough light and space for everyone. As you might expect from a proprietor in his 20s, Hush is inventive, nicely kooky and uses a wedge of reclaimed material while keeping the nice period bits (ceiling moldings, parquet) in place – items that would be wrenched from their place in the rest of modern Turkey. The bar also holds temporary exhibitions for upcoming Turkish artists, of which much stays on display, hopefully forever more. A quiet upstairs salon and a leafy garden complete the mix.

Isis (left)
Kadife Sokak 26, Kadiköy
Tel: 00 90 216 349 7381
www.isisrest.com
Open: daily, 9am–2am

Set on Kadiköy's prime street for intoxication, Kadife Sokak, Isis is a bar-cum-dance venue in an old three-storey house. A mild Egyptian theme sets the visual tone with murals and statuary but happily doesn't spill over into the programming of the live music or to all of the funky indoor drinking areas. The patio/garden at the back, with tiled and wooden flooring, is absolutely massive and you can hear a collective sigh of relief as pints are put to lips on warm summer evenings. All in all, Isis is a justifiably popular boozer with those in their 20s and 30s. Its menu has expanded in recent years to include pizzas, supersize salads and lazy breakfasts.

The James Joyce (right)
Balo Sokak 26, Beyoğlu
Tel: 00 90 212 244 7970
www.theirishcentre.com
Open: daily, 10am–2am

The James Joyce – Istanbul's only Irish pub and a surprisingly enormous establishment opposite the bottom of Nevizarde Sokak – is popular with the full variety of English-speaking ex-pats and locals. As expected, Irish clichés are on display, including fading posters of James Joyce's Dublin and portraits of Oscar Wilde (who, we firmly believe, would have hated the place). Snobs like Wilde aside, it's fun, obviously casual and occupies a very pretty building (the pub's unexpected library is very nice – though low on books). And if you suddenly become bored with Turkish culture you can take advantage of the pub's raft of regular Irish activities including Irish music sessions, Irish film club meetings and salsa dancing (?). An all-day Irish breakfast of bacon, sausages, eggs, mushrooms, tomatoes and chips will set you up for the day.

K.V. (bottom)
Tünel Geçidi 10, Beyoğlu
Tel: 00 90 212 251 4338
Open: daily, 8am–2am

At the bottom Sofayalı Sokak you can find a glimpse of Old Constantinople in the form of Hacer Gündoğdu's restaurant and coffee house, K.V. A decorative, wrought-iron gate opens onto a passage filled with tables interspersed with tall, abundant plants, an area that is especially beautiful at night when it is subtly and quite magically lit. Inside the

old 19th-century building Gündoğdu, who owns the next-door antique shop Artrium, has decorated the rooms to recall the Viennese and Parisian styles once so common in the area. Cabinets full of antique bottles, odd examples of Victorian clothing, ancient telephones and other curiosities conjure a comforting nostalgic air, which means that K.V. is as enchanting in winter as it is in summer. Happily, despite the historical touches and central location, it attracts a mixed bag of locals more than tourists.

Kino Garden   *(left)*
Sofayalı Sokak 4, Asmalımescit
Tel: 00 20 212 245 0010
Open: noon–midnight. Closed Sundays.

Drinkers at Kino are as likely to be wielding a paintbrush, tape recorder or something else creative-industries related as they are a gin and tonic or Caipiroska. This is a lovely little bar – as popular with daytime design meetings as it is with evening revellers – in the middle of the Asmalımescit hotspot, pulling in a fashionable crowd, generally in their mid-20s and -30s. Its interior is tiny, decorated with painted murals and retro-patterned furniture; outside is a smallish but lovely garden shrouded in fairy lights that is extremely popular on warm evenings.

Leb-i-Derya   *(bottom)*
Kumbaracı Yokuşu 57, Tünel
Tel: 00 90 212 293 4989
www.lebiderya.com
Open: 5pm–2am Mon–Fri,
10am–3am Sat & Sun.

The main attraction for the smart Is-

tanbul set who frequent Leb-i-Derya is themselves. By rights, though, it should be the views, which pan out over Europe's biggest metropolis, and are almost good enough to fall into when the summer terrace opens up in summer. On the top floor of a tall, early 20th-century building just off Istiklal Caddesi, Leb-i-Derya was renovated in light, woody contemporary tones after a destructive fire some years ago – a scary thought this high up. The cocktails served by the lovely staff are innovative and include basil margarita, hazelnut vodka and the rather terrifying-sounding gin strike. They all pack a punch and strangely seem to get better as the evening wears on, peaking in the very small hours.

Limonlu Bahçe   *(right)*
Yenicarsı Caddesi 98, Galatasaray
Tel: 00 90 212 252 1094
Open: daily, 9.30am–1am

After ducking and diving through a few doorways and passages off the steep slope of Yenicarsı Caddesi, you'll find yourself in the very pleasant, big back garden that is Limonlu Bahçe – the Lemon Garden. The atmosphere on a sultry summer eve is divine, like stepping into a tranquil Moorish garden. Comfy pillows and cushions, hammocks and casual (in every sense) staff – which present an excellent haven from the noisy bustle of Istiklal Caddesi – no doubt assist the scene. A cool crowd in their 20s and 30s fills the place in the evenings and weekends, though it's generally quiet on weekdays. Though an increasing trend, gardens are pretty rare in this quarter of Istanbul, and Limonlu Bahçe

drink…

is particularly nice. But be warned: it may be lovely for a drink, but the food won't win awards anytime soon.

Lokal *(left)*
Mueyyet Sokak 9, Tünel
Tel: 00 90 212 245 4028
www.lokal-istanbul.com
Open: daily, 8am–midnight (1am Fri/Sat)

Trend-central, as you can tell from the vintage Turkish tiled floors and the knowingly kitsch, retro decoration, Lokal is small but immensely popular with the city's young and hip. Being handily located just off Istiklal and Sofayali Sokak helps. The food is global, prepared in an open kitchen, varying from good, fresh, homemade burgers to Pad Thai via every other culinary country going. There is often a riotous atmosphere here as Lokal is something of a meeting point for a familiar, friendly crowd – it can get quite boisterous, especially as the cocktails are good. Art house films are projected onto the alley wall opposite the bar come eve; a top place for brunch and breakfast, too.

Nu Teras *(right)*
Meflrutiyet Caddesi 67, Beyoğlu
Tel: 00 90 212 245 6070
www.nupera.com.tr
Open: daily, 6pm–1am (4am Fri/Sat).

Around sunset in summer there are few places more (literally) dazzlingly spectacular to have a drink than Nu Teras, a smooth, ultra-cool bar atop an elegant seven-storey, 19th-century building in Pera. As if designed with an astronomical precision that would put the architects of Stonehenge to shame (the owners may have just struck lucky, of course), Nu Teras is perfectly aligned with the setting sun so that as it falls it spills out, reflecting on the sleek, smoked glass bar and the shiny table-tops. Accordingly, it's one of the few places where sunglasses are actually a medical necessity rather than a fashion faux pas. DJs spin away as you sip your cocktails and watch Istanbul's beautiful crowd file in. Nu Teras is more than a bar, though, being the summer berth for an al fresco restaurant that dishes up sharing platters, pizzas, dips, organic breads and chops, which makes it hard to leave even after the sun has set.

Pia *(bottom)*
Bekar Sokak 6, off Istiklal Caddesi, Beyoğlu
Tel: 00 90 212 252 7100
Open: daily, 3pm–2am

Though small, Pia, just off the Taksim end of Istiklal, manages to exude a good deal of atmosphere. It attracts a regular and select crowd of locals as well as its fair share of passing tourists drawn in by its warm, wood-panelled walls and ornate mirrors. Pia has a reputation for being frequented by attractive women, promulgated by previous guidebooks, which counterproductively encourages solitary, male foreigners to flock to the bar and scare off the aforementioned attractive women. You must therefore discourage such rumours even if you happen to find them to be true. A small, summer-only terrace adds to the cosiness.

drink...

Sensus Turkish Wine Library
(top)

Büyükhendek Caddesi 5, Galata
Tel: 00 90 212 245 5657
www.sensuswine.com
Open: daily, 10am–10pm

A brilliant new addition to the Galata bar scene, Sensus calls itself 'a wine and cheese boutique'. It's actually a shop-cum-tasting salon where visitors can imbibe more than 350 types of Turkish wines, often in batches of 10 or 20, or just sup a few glasses for a quick foray into eastern viticulture. Rare for Turkey, there's a wide selection of local cheeses also on offer, and can be tagged on to a *degustation du vin* for just a few extra lira. The cellar is rather medieval and offers cool respite from the summer heat – and remains at a great temperature for serious wine tasting of rarer vintages.

Sultan Pub
(top-right)

Divan Yolu 2, Sultanahmet
Tel: 00 90 212 528 1719
www.sultanpub.com.tr
Open: daily, 8am–2am

Sultanahmet is not blessed with a profusion of elegant bars. So unless you want to relive your backpacking days – in which case there is plenty of choice – the Sultan Pub, among a few others, makes a nice bet. Suffering something of a multi-personality disor-

der – Laurel & Hardy statuettes meet French bistro chic – the Sultan Pub has a nice European café-style spread of tables while inside on the ground floor is an American-inspired bar with slatted blinds and neon signs. Upstairs is a roof terrace, with – yes – lovely views of the historic old city, while there's an additional garden terrace out front complete with waiter service.

....

Taps *(bottom-right)*
Cevdetpaşa Caddesi 119, Bebek
Tel: 00 90 212 263 8700
www.tapsistanbul.com
Open: daily, 11.30am–1am (2am Fri/Sat)

Istanbul's first micro-brewery is about

the only place in town to go if you're a beer fanatic and have developed a dislike for the ubiquitous Efes pilsener. It brews seven (tasty) beers in total, including a flowery wheat beer and a complex award-winning ale. Located in the smart suburb of Bebek, it appeals to a youthful, upmarket crowd eager to fill the trendiest venues possible. Taps, happy to reciprocate, signals its fashionability with lots of stainless steel, exposed ventilation systems and diner-style booths. The relationship is consummated for both parties over the relatively pricey food and drink. Clearly someone's doing something right as the place is packed most of the time.

....

Urban *(top)*
Kartal Sokak 6 (off Istiklal
Caddesi), Beyoğlu
Tel: 00 90 212 252 1325
www.urbanbeyoglu.com
Open: daily, 11am–1am

A hip dive bar – for want of a better explanation – that in good Istanbul fashion serves decent food as well. Its interior has an attractive Parisian feel to it, perfect for a lazy breakfast or afternoon coffee lingering over the paper, while outside a small terrace-like set-up of tables is shaded by leafy creepers that climb over the iron climbing frame. A popular venue with slightly older sophisticated media and cultural types, Urban is often used as a starting-point for an evening's adventure. The especially nice staff deserves a mention, too.

Yesil Ev Garden *(bottom)*
Kabasakal Caddesi 5,
Sultanahmet
Tel: 00 90 212 517 6785
www.yesilev.com.tr
Open: daily, 10am–11pm

An elegant option within sight of the Hagia Sophia, the bucolic Yesil Ev Garden is one of the few places in Sultanahmet that one can recommend as a good place for a drink. An ornate fountain burbles away in the centre of the stone-flagged garden, which is surrounded by tulips in spring and shaded by a number of tall, mature trees (an endangered species in central Istanbul). The wrought-iron garden furniture, matching streetlamps and bow-tied staff give the place a turn of the last century ambience.

The garden is just as nice for a daytime tea or coffee as it is for a cooling lager or a glass of white wine after a hard day's sightseeing in the Old City.

URBAN

snack…

There are few cities where the street food is as cheap, plentiful or as good as here. Hawkers with their mobile units sell boiled or grilled corn-on-the-cobs and rice-stuffed mussels all over town. In most areas you don't have to go far to find a *kebabçi* or *köfteci*, where the traditional and uncomplicated fare of a plate of *köfte* (spiced, grilled meatballs) is served with side orders of rice, salad and *ayran*, the local beloved salty yoghurt drink. For a traditional taste, try Tarihi Selim Usta Sultanahmet Köftecisi on Divan Yolu in the heart of Sultanahmet, or indeed the countless, nameless others. However, it's best to avoid the more obviously touristy joints in picture-postcard areas where the relationship between the cook and his art is loveless, dictated by money, expediency and circumstance.

Other traditional pleasures are to be found at Vefa Bozacısı, near the Grand Bazaar, which serves up *boza*, a nourishing, fermented millet drink, and *şıra*, a fizzy grape juice. Also indigenous is the *nargile*, or hookah. Of course, smoking a 'hubbly bub-bly' is considered to be the height of hippy naffness in the West, and for most of the 20th-century a self-respecting Turk would have agreed, bracketing it along with fez-wearing in the highest category of cultural no-nos. Now the *nargile* has made a comeback. Visit the *nargile* cafés in Tophane or head to Erenler Çay Bahçesi, next door to the Grand Bazaar, and you'll find more locals than visitors.

An altogether different world is on view at the many fashionable cafés that pepper the smart and wealthy areas of Nisantısı and the Bosphorus villages. At Beyman Brasserie and Armani Café, you can swap the thick Turkish coffees for espressos and a feigned air of boredom. A younger, but similarly well-heeled crowd flocks to the cafés in and around Ortaköy and Bebek, with Bosphorus-side Aşşk Café, Mangerie and the House Café especially popular.

Back in the more artsy neighbourhoods of Beyoğlu there is a different vibe yet again. In Galata, Mavra is both a design workshop and a café, mixing homemade meals with crafty creations. White Mill Café and Symrna are local hotspots in Ci-hangir, happily offering tasty food and drink all day long. Nearby, Van Kahvaltı Evi dishes up particularly tasty breakfasts, while Cuppa blends an amazing range of organic smoothies and Miss Pizza fires up the best pizzas in town. In Asmalımescit, Şimdi offers strong Italian coffee and a varied menu. Around the corner on Istiklal Caddesi, Markiz Café, with its gorgeous Art Nouveau tiled panels depicting the seasons, is a reminder of Beyoğlu's chic, cosmopolitan past. So too is the Pera Palace, where afternoon tea in the famous Kubbeli Saloon is a reminder of its early 20th-century heyday.

Patisserie de Pera

Armani Cafe *(top)*
İstinye Bayırı Caddesi, İstinye
Park Alışveriş Merkezi, İstinye
Tel: 00 90 212 345 6140
Open: daily, 10am–midnight

The northern neighbourhoods of Istanbul – including Nisantası, Teş vikiye and İstinye – are unashamedly obsessed with beautiful people. If you're browsing the area's designer labels, why not head straight to the spiritual home of style, Armani Cafe? Perched above İstinye Park's Emporio Armani store, the café's Italian food is both fashionable and beautifully presented, as are the staff and the customers. Stop in for a coffee, savour a light lunch or spoil yourself with a truffle, porcini and Parmesan evening extravaganza. Saturdays throughout winter are celebrated with special happy-hour cocktails.

Aşşk Kahve *(middle)*
Muallim Naci Caddesi 64/B,
Kuruçeşme
Tel: 0212 265 4734
www.asskkahve.com
Open: daily, 10am–11pm (1am Apr–Oct)

Aşşk Kahve is a cute Bosphorus-side café, just north of the glitzy club and bar strip of Kuruçeşme. A hangout where the trendy and beautiful go to top up their tans, it's a magnet for the models, footballers and celeb wannabes who pass their days here, sipping espressos, nibbling the regionally-inspired salads or reading the papers over long, lingering weekend breakfasts. And you certainly can't fault their choice of venue. Despite being hidden behind a supermarket, Aşşk (meaning love) is superbly located right on the waterfront and benefits from a sprinkling of shade-giving trees, making it positively idyllic on a sunny day. Though a destination in itself, at night it's also a good place to pop in for a drink before hitting the nearby clubs.

Bambi *(bottom)*
Sıraselviler Caddesi 14
(among others), Taksim
Tel: 00 90 212 292 3406
Open: daily, 24 hours

Back home when you get drunk and end up gorging on that near-fatal kebab after a night out you know that there will be no excuses good enough to assuage the guilt and shame that comes the following day. Here at least you can file the event as an authentic cultural experience, especially if you head to fast-food outlet Bambi on the corner of Taksim Square: the café is something of an Istanbullu institution, having served kebabs 24 hours a day since 1974. Its popularity is clearly demonstrated by its extraordinary and slightly sinister expansion down Sıraselviler Caddesi, occupying as it does a string of shop fronts. Providing excellent material for field research in anthropological studies on intoxicated Turks (if you're lucky a fight might break out), a trip to Bambi also offers cheap, fast and reliable kebabs.

Bej Kahve *(left)*
Kemankeş Caddesi, Fransız
Geçidi İş Merkezi 11/A, Karaköy
Tel: 00 90 212 251 7195
Open: daily, 8am–7pm Mon–Sat,
10am–4pm Sun

Tucked into Karaköy's 'French Passageway', Bej Kahve is the cosiest new café in this increasingly gentrified neighbourhood. The open plan space is edged by a long bar, and the jazzy music and fresh flowers that grace each table lend a touch of Paris to the place. Menu items concentrate on seasonal soups, wraps and bountiful salads (salmon sashimi in Asian dressing or roasted beet paired with chunks of goat's cheese), and there's always a two-course daily set menu on offer.

Post-dining, circle around the café's central island to check out the cards, recycled old school paper notebooks and unusual bags at Kağıthane, a stationary and gift store that shares the premises.

....

Beymen Brasserie *(middle)*
Abdi İpekçi Caddesi 23/1,
Nişantaşi
Tel: 00 90 212 343 0444
Open: daily, 10am–11pm

Vying with Armani Café for the best place in Istanbul to lunch while looking elegant, this smooth brasserie located on the ground floor of Beymen's slickest store was designed by renowned local architect, Zeynep Fadıllıoğlu. The gleaming wooden bar and soft

leather bucket seats compliment the Art Deco feel, while the commendable coffee and its pricey Mediterranean menu prove that the store's beautiful customers don't survive on light and expensive products alone. Big windows allow everyone to be seen. It's not cheap, but nor is the company.

Bistro *(right)*
inside SALT Beyoğlu,
Istiklal Caddesi 136, Beyoğlu
Tel: 00 90 212 251 6628
www.bistro.com.tr
Open: noon–midnight. Closed Mondays

Bistro is the latest chic outpost from famed Istanbullu foodie Murat Bozok, the head chef at Mimolett. Since mid-2011 it has sat in plum position in the tranquil surrounds of the all-new SALT Beyoğlu art space, a beguilingly beautiful cultural institution in the middle of Istiklal Caddesi. This sleek offering is centred around an open bar and kitchen, while dotted around are tables full of foodie books, booths with plush banquettes and seriously designer tables and chairs. The same seating arrangement continues outside in a courtyard all summer long in a spot that soaks up the last of the evening sun. As the name suggests, Bistro dishes up simple, hearty, tasty meals with a handy open-all-hours service. Prices are up there with the best of them, though – glasses of tea are a rather silly 5TL – although the 6–8pm happy hour pulls in punters for half-price beers in the sun.

Café di Dolce *(left)*
Kuruçeşme Caddesi 25, Kuruçeşme
Tel: 00 90 212 257 7299
www.alladolce.com
Open: 9am–6pm. Closed Sundays

If you fancy a fabulous cake and you're somewhere in the Bosphorus vicinity, then dropping in for a quick sugar fix at Café di Dolce is a must. In the tiny, pretty, green and beige café, owner, former model and current cakemaster Nilgün Ertug struts her stuff before your very eyes, baking as she serves. Charm your companion with one of Nilgün's distinctive heart- or shooting star-shaped biscuits. Café di Dolce also prepares bespoke cakes and sandwiches, as well as cater-

ing for weddings and special events.

Cuppa *(middle)*
Yeni Yuva Sokak 26/5, Cihangir
Tel: 00 90 212 249 5723
www.cuppajuice.com
Open: daily, 9am–10pm

Packed with slim ladies, glowing yogis and a good sprinkling of resident expats, laid-back Cuppa is the best spot in the city for a serious smoothie. Make the force yours via Jedi Juice (pineapple, pear, grape and apple), kill a hangover with Detox Juice (apple, orange, carrot and wheatgrass) or plump for the local specialty, Istanbul Juice (apple, kiwi and banana). Cuppa also

serves excellent breakfasts, brunches and big organic salads; the relaxed atmosphere and free WiFi make it great for whiling away a lazy afternoon.

Enstitü *(right)*
Istanbul Culinary Istitute,
Mesrutiyet Caddesi 59, Tepebasi
Tel: 00 90 212 251 2214
www.istanbulculinary.com
Open: 7.30am–6pm Mon–Fri;
8am–5pm Sat.

A 'practice restaurant' for the on-site Istanbul Culinary Institute, Enstitü serves regional Turkish specialties, adding a unique contemporary or Mediterranean twist to each one.

There are always both daily and monthly menus, highlighting seasonal delights (broad bean soup, quince compote, sweet watermelon and feta cheese), and tasting menus (paired with Turkish wines) are frequently on offer. Look out for outstanding homemade breads – in particular the crumbly corn one. Although the restaurant menu is cooked in full by head chef Bülent Metin and the students enrolled in Chefschool, the school's professional cooking courses, the Institute also offers short English-language workshops and culinary tours of the city geared towards foodie-obsessed visitors.

Erenler Aile Çay Bahçesi *(left)*
Çorlulu Ali Paşa Medresesi 36/28,
Yeniçeriler Caddesi, Beyazit
Tel: 00 90 212 511 8853
Open: daily, 7am–midnight
(until 3am in the summer).

Nargile (hookah) smoking, callow-pretentious student-style naffness in the West, was, until recently, just lamely old-fashioned in Turkey. Now it's going through a resurgence, which means your obligatory *nargile* experience won't be as embarrassing as it would have been even a few years ago. Symptomatic of this casual movement of the fickle hand of fashion is the breakdown of the customers at Erenler Aile Çay Bahçesi, who, despite being right next to the Grand Bazaar, are more local than foreign. Set in the atmospheric courtyard of an old Ottoman seminary, it's a good place to be, especially as dusk falls. Sip tea and fill up on toasted cheese sandwiches. For a trendier *nargile* experience, try the numerous beanbag-decked cafés that cluster together off Tophane Iskelesi behind the Nusretiye Mosque, near the Bosphorus waterfront in the southeast of Beyoğlu.

The Four *(bottom)*
Seasons' Lounge
Tevkifhane Sokak 1, Sultanahmet
Tel: 00 40 212 402 3000
www.fourseasons.com/istanbul
Open: daily, 11am–11.30pm
(3–6pm afternoon tea).

One of only two spots in Istanbul that offer an equivalent of high tea at the Ritz (the other being the Kubbeli Saloon at the Pera Palace), The Four Seasons' Lounge is spread over a casual mix of lush winter gardens and shady courtyard pergolas. And despite the lack of one specific grand dining room, the exquisite afternoon tea service is as formal as one would expect (and obviously as pricey, too). The freshly-made sandwiches, French pastries and biscuits are all impeccable.

House Café *(right)*
Teşvikiye Caddesi 146, Nişantaşi
Tel: 00 90 212 327 1774
www.thehousecafe.com
Open: daily, 8am–1am (2am Fri/Sat,
midnight Sun)

The super trendy House Café has a dozen branches dotted around town, including locales in Ortaköy, Tünel and Nişantaşı. The latter is a lovely domed corner café with its own back garden; the Ortaköy branch is a good stop if you're trawling along the Bosphorus near the clubs of Kuruçeşme. All boast large wooden tables, minimalistic cool décor and a loyal following among Istanbul's fashionable crowd. All the girls look immaculate and sport identical haircuts and accessories, which must make it confusing for the tanned, affluent-looking open-shirted men who hang around trying to get them drunk (best to go to Ortaköy if you want to take part in this kind of thing). Everything's moderately expensive by Istanbul standards. The cocktails are good, as is the food, which is standard cool café fare – pizzas, pastas and salads. The burger is something of a speciality and is comes highly recommended. At evenings and weekends in the summer the House Café in Ortaköy gets especially packed so be sure to book ahead if you plan to dine here.

snack.....

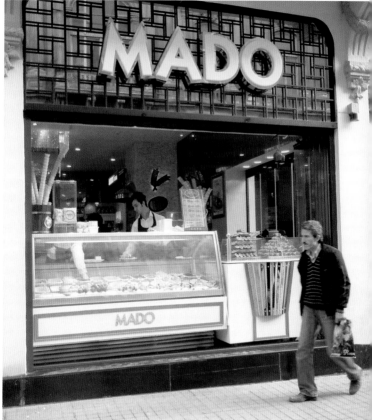

Karaköy Güllüoğlu *(left)*
Mumhane Caddesi 171, Karaköy
Tel: 00 90 212 293 0910
www.karakoygulluoglu.com
Open: 8am–7pm. Closed Sundays.

Follow Istanbul's Turkish tourists who make a beeline to this spot of *baklava* pilgrimage, emerging with box upon box of goodies for friends and family back home. This waterside neighbourhood has been synonymous with baklava since 1949, when Mustafa Güllü left his native Gaziantep to open up his own shop here. Today, Karaköy Güllüoğlu's specialties remain walnut and pistachio *baklava*, created by interspersing dozens of famously ultra-light layers of pastry with butter and nuts. The *börek* – savoury pastry stuffed with spinach, cheese, potatoes or beef – makes for a very tasty, speedy breakfast, too.

Kiva Han *(right)*
Galata Kulesi Meydanı 4,
Galata, Beyoğlu
Tel: 00 90 212 292 9898
www.galatakivahan.com
Open: daily, 9am–midnight

Nudged up against the base of the Galata Tower, Kiva Han's sunny terrace is perfect for Sunday brunch or an evening meal away from the more obvious nighttime spots around nearby Asmalımescit. The bustling restaurant serves up innovative versions of traditional pan-Anatolian recipes (meatballs in cool cucumber mint *cacık*), as well as a tasty range of veggie options (stuffed courgettes, or cumin-spiked bulgur *köfte*), daily soups and an open *meze* buffet. And if you find the menu totally baffling, there's a selection of daily dishes that can be chosen by pointing at the hot trays inside. Turkish coffee and tea have been joined lately by filter coffee and other Euro-style caffeine options, and while it may appear that Kiva Han doesn't serve alcohol, just ask for a wine or beer and it will arrive in an undercover coffee mug.

Mado Ice Cream *(bottom)*
İstiklal Caddesi 121
(among others), Beyoğlu
Tel: 00 90 212 245 4631
www.mado.com.tr
Open: most of the time.

With outlets all over the city, Mado is Istanbul's (and Turkey's) favourite ice-cream brand and parlour chain. Its gloopy, almost chewy wares are mixed up the traditional Turkish way, using goat's milk, sugar and salep, a powder made from ground wild orchid tubers. The latter allegedly possesses aphrodisiacal powers, which perhaps adds to the enormous popularity of Turkish ice-cream. There is an array of more than 80 flavours on offer, including date, pomegranate, fig, carrot, pumpkin and fabulously rich dark chocolate.

snack…

119

Mangerie *(top)*
*Cevdet Paşa Caddesi 69
(3rd Floor), Bebek
Tel: 00 90 212 263 5199
www.mangeriebebek.com
Open: daily, 8am–midnight*

A terrace floor in an old, wooden apartment building in Bebek forms the setting for one of the loveliest café-restaurants in the city. The light colour scheme complements the place's period features; meanwhile, you can sit back and observe as your meal is prepared in the open kitchen. Breakfast, lunches and dinners are all good here (and not too formal), and you can stop in for a coffee or a pitcher of one of the house cocktails and enjoy the chic company. Note that this spot is one of the few places in Istanbul that serves decent bacon, so it's worth the trip if you're missing your porky fry-ups (which are served via elegant Eggs Benedict and the like). The only drawback, from your point of view is that Mangerie is in Bebek, and you probably aren't.

Markiz Café *(left)*
*İstiklal Caddesi 362,
Beyoğlu
Tel: 00 90 212 244 9039
Open: daily, 9am–10pm*

A survivor from the Pera neighbourhood's glamorous heyday, the Markiz was saved from dereliction and spruced up by the owners of the Richmond Hotel across the street. Despite the probable press of tourists you'll encounter, it's worth a visit to sit and enjoy the tiled Art Noveau wall designs of French artist J.A. Arnoux, which depict spring and autumn (the other two seasons were lost somewhere along the way). During the early 20th-century, members of Istanbul's intelligentsia and artistic community frequented the Markiz. They were attracted to the café primarily for its renowned pastries (baked in the special pastry oven the Markiz's original owners shipped over from Paris) and by each other's sophisticated company. The pastries are still good, as are the coffees. Sadly, atmosphere is rather harder to restore.

Mavra *(right)*

*Serdar Ekrem Caddesi 31/A,
Galata, Beyoğlu
Tel: 00 90 212 252 7488
Open: daily, 8am–midnight*

Part hipster café, part design workshop, Marva is one of Galata's coolest neighbourhood hangouts. A mix of local artists and students sprawl over the wide tables, flicking through design magazines or using the free WiFi, set against a backdrop of funky tunes. The café's walls are used to display the crafty works currently on sale, and are frequently clad in quilted cushions, chunky jewellery and prints, while the beautiful old tiled floors add a touch of Turkish tradition. Homemade soups, sandwiches and cakes are served throughout the day, and there's an open buffet brunch on weekends. Delightfully non-posy.

snack...

LE PRINTEMPS

 **Meşale Çay Bahçesi** *(top)*
Arasta Bazaar 45, Sultanahmet
Tel: 00 90 212 518 9562
Open: daily, 24 hours

Occupying a corner of the Blue Mosque's complex of buildings at the end of the Arasta Bazaar, Meşale is an atmospheric sunken teahouse. Post-sightseeing, it makes an ideal spot to rest underneath the shady awnings, have a nargile, drink or snack. Unsurprisingly, its location means it's ever popular with tourists, though in the evening workers from local shops and businesses come here, too. There's traditional live music, as well as Dervish performances most nights.

 Miss Pizza *(middle-left)*
*Akarsu Caddesi, Havyar
Sokak 5/A, Cihangir*
Tel: 00 90 212 251 3278
Open: daily, noon–10.30pm

If you get tired of the *meze*, kebabs and so on, you can fill up on the lovely wood-oven-baked pizzas at the popular and perenially packed Miss Pizza: be sure to reserve or get here early to secure a table. The owners have a dab hand at manipulating styles and fashions, so it's hard to tell whether the joint's décor is super-subtle kitsch or just economical; either way it looks like a little slice of stereotypical Italy in Istanbul, with red-and-white check as the dominant motif. An additional branch of Miss Pizza recently opened at Meşrutiyet Caddesi, Tepe Han 86/A, Şişhane, near the İstiklal Caddesi Tünel funicular stop.

 Nature & Peace *(middle-right)*
*İstiklal Caddesi, Büyük
Parmakkapı Sokak 15/A, Beyoğlu*
Tel: 00 90 212 245 8609
www.natureandpeace.com
Open: daily, 11am (1pm Fri/Sat)
–11.30pm

Nature & Peace was one of Istanbul's first restaurants aimed at vegetarians in the city. Recently rounding out 15 thriving years, the owners have now made a slight foray into the world of chicken and fish, presumably because strict vegetarians are so rare here. Nevertheless, the family-run eatery has a good, healthy menu, including bags of pulses, rice and beans. There are also creative takes on traditionally meaty Turkish dishes, such as veggie *mantı* (mince-stuffed pasta in garlic yogurt sauce) and meat-free *köfte* (meatballs).

 Küçük Otto *(bottom)*
*Şehbender Sokak 5/1,
Asmalımescit, Tünel*
Tel: 00 90 212 292 7015
www.ottoistanbul.com
Open: 3pm–4am. Closed Sundays.

A popular spot near Tünel, Otto dishes up simple but tasty Italian pizzas, pastas and Turkish-style tapas – which means this in-the-know joint has fast become a neighbourhood favourite. The restaurant's interior is inviting, a punky mix of tiled surfaces, graffiti, lanterns and stacks of logs ready to fuel the proper pizza oven. Wine-sipping patrons often crowd the bar, and the whole haunt turns into a tiny club around midnight on weekends. There are two other Ottos in town, too: nearby at Sofyalı Sokak

snack...

22/A, and further afield at santralistanbul, Kazım Karabekir Caddesi 2/7.

....

Patisserie de Pera *(top)*
*Kubbeli Saloon Tea Lounge
& Orient Terrace Bar, Pera Palace,
Meşrutiyet Caddesi 52, Tepebaşı
Tel: 00 90 212 377 4000
www.perapalace.com
Open: daily, 8am–9pm*

Few hotels can boast the range and quality of roles in fiction that the Pera Palace has on its CV, popping up as it does in Agatha Christie's Murder on the Orient Express, Ian Fleming's From Russia with Love and Alfred Hitchcock's The Lady Vanishes. Even if you don't opt to bed down here, there are still plenty of ways to savour the hotel's literature-soaked ambience. Patisserie de Pera, the elegant and charming in-house patisserie, serves French pastries, macaroons and pots of coffee in grand hotel style. Alternatively, book a table in the Kubbeli Saloon for afternoon tea, where the lavish buffet is overflowing with cucumber and salmon sandwiches, berry tarts, chocolate cake and similar. If an evening aperitif appeals, the Orient Terrace Bar – with views over the Golden Horn – is ideal for a sundowner or an evening snack. The only blot on these particular landscapes is the number of tourists you'll find there clutching, er... guidebooks, and spoiling the atmosphere (so hide the book and try not to look like a tourist. Elegant late 19th-century period dress should do it).

....

Pierre Loti Kahvesi *(bottom)*
*Gümüşsuyu Caddesi,
Balmumcu Sokak 5, Eyüp
Tel: 00 90 212 581 2696
Open: daily, 9am–9pm*

Really this entry is just an excuse for us to tell you about Pierre Loti (1850–1923, real name Julien Viand). Sadly, the unabashedly romantic and Orientalist French novelist is largely forgotten, his prose being a little too purple for modern taste. Except, that is, among the Turks, who love him for the very good reason that he loved them. Here's Pierre waxing lyrical about Istanbul in his novel Les Désenchantées: 'As he felt deeply Turkish on this warm, clear evening... on the familiar esplanade in front of the Sultan Fatih's mosque. He wanted to dream there, in the pure cool of the evening, and in the sweet Oriental peace, smoking hookahs while surrounded by dying splendour, decay, religious silence and prayer'. As for the Pierre Loti café, it's situated northwest of the Old City at the top of a leafy hill above the Eyüp Sultan Cemetery, with unrivalled views over the Golden Horn and the city's magnificent skyline. The management tentatively suggests that it might have been this café that Loti visited while staying in Eyüp in 1876. This claim may be the sort of thing medieval monks said about their saint's relics, hoping to draw in the punters while knowing very well that their holy bones belonged to a sheep that died of the plague a few decades earlier. Nevertheless, it's a quiet, calm, bucolic place of which Loti would have approved (but he would have hated the modern development, also called Pierre Loti, where your taxi may drop

you off – head down the gravel path to the old tea garden).

....

Şimdi *(top)*
Asmalımescit Sokak,
Atlas Apt 5, Tünel
Tel: 00 90 212 252 5443
Open: daily, 8am–1am

A cosy option for a coffee and a snack if you're around the Tünel end of Istiklal Caddesi is the casually elegant Şimdi (meaning 'Now'), with its Illy coffee, lovely modern chandelier and attractive blue tiling. On warm days the sliding doors are pulled back so that the comfortable front section is exposed to the street, where bench seats make a great people-watching spot. The back eating area includes a space that is effectively a courtyard, open to the sky and surrounded on all sides by the windows of the flats above. The long menu is simple (pastas, salads, sandwiches) and includes tasty (Turkish-style) breakfast options; there's also a good selection of wines by the glass, and free WiFi, too.

....

Smyrna *(middle)*
Akarsu Caddesi 29, Cihangir
Tel: 00 90 212 244 2466
Open: 10am–2am. Closed Mondays.

An enduring hub for Cihangir's hip social scene, Smyrna is a former antiques shop-turned-buzzing neighbourhood bar. The retro tone is set at the entrance with an eclectic collection of bric-à-brac, dolls, typewriters, old bottles and so on. The rest of the décor is similarly mixed-up, with lots of comfortable old sofas and armchairs. The clientele would like to be eclectic, too, but they're all arty types (and so constitute a social monoculture, even if it's a creative one). The food and drink, served all day and into the night, is good, though priced more in line with central London than local Istanbul (but you're paying for the cool). There's even a super comfortable tiny platform area accessible by a steep set of ladder-steps where you can have a lounge or a lie-down, and the relaxed staff probably won't mind if you doze off (as long as you keep ordering food and drink in your sleep).

....

Sugar Club Café *(bottom)*
Sakasalim Çıkmazı 3/A, Beyoğlu
Tel: 00 90 212 245 0096
www.sugar-cafe.com
Open: daily, 11am–1am

Down a small side street off İstiklal Caddesi is the Sugar Club Café, a tiny, unpretentious, contemporary spot, and one of the only openly gay daytime venues in the city. Serving a nice cup of coffee and food cooked up by owner-chef Murat Sögütlüoglu, Sugar Club Café is a welcoming spot for those seeking refuge from the crowds along İstiklal Caddesi. Fairly quiet during the day, it picks up in the evening with live music and people spilling out onto the little backstreet. The chatty staff encourages you to ask about the local gay nightlife, or feel free to ply them with any other questions you may have about gay life in Istanbul.

....

party...

Unabashed hedonists, the Turks' sincere enjoyment of the pleasures of the table is only equalled by their appreciation of drinking, dancing and showing off. Accordingly, Istanbul's nightclub scene is both dense and varied.

At the glittering, conspicuous consumption end of the market, Istanbul's clubs effortlessly match their Mediterranean rivals in St. Tropez and Beirut, albeit with a less international clientele. With their own significant tranche of the super-rich – only Moscow, New York, London and Hong Kong have more billionaires than Istanbul – the Turks haven't yet got round to importing other peoples'.

An improbably large hoarding erected over the entrance to Reina, the city's premier super-club, sets the none-too-subtle tone for a string of clubs, including Sortie and Angelique, which sit on the shore of the Bosphorus in Kuruçeşme just a short drive from Beyoğlu. In summer they are, for an assorted collection of moguls, Mafiosi, models, wannabe models, footballers, miscellaneously rich and curious foreigners, the place to be seen.

Place, singular, since, in the spirit of a corporate marketing exercise, the glitterati tend to maximise their visibility by visiting as many clubs in one night as is humanly possible. The interchangeability of the venues is underscored by their regular attention-seeking name changes. Sited on the shoreline, the clubs afford their clients spectacular views and, for the really flashy, the chance to avoid queues by docking their yachts at their very own piers. Extraordinarily large, they tend to house a range of restaurants, bars and dance-floors, so that, technically, you need never leave, though on a practical level that would lead to the rapid implosion of your wallet. Off-season, the clubs either move to venues in town or take a tax-efficient break.

Back in town, 360° sits loftily above Istiklal Caddesi, and is one of the cooler alternatives to the Bosphorus clubs. Babylon, in Asmalımescit, is the city's top music venue, attracting international DJs and guitar bands. If in the mood for something more sedate, the excellent Nardis Jazz Club is the best place to sample Istanbul's surprisingly thriving jazz scene. The city's clutch of newer, more offbeat clubs has found a home in Beyoğlu too, including Riddim for hip-hop and Indigo for electronica.

Istanbul's attitude towards sex and sexuality is somewhat ambivalent. Turkey's metropolitan elites are proud of the country's secularity, something of a modern extension of Ottoman traditional broadmindedness that is typified in a speech Mehmet the Conqueror delivered to his troops during their siege of Constantinople. When the usual promises of plunder and female virgins on victory proved insufficiently moving, he hastily tacked on: 'And you will have boys, too, very many and very beautiful and of noble families.' The city fell the next day. Though homophobia is far from extinct, the gay scene is active and Sugar Club Café (see Snack) is a good place to start. There is also a small but highly visible transvestite population, who are a world and law unto themselves (and hang out in the backstreets around Taksim, if you're asking).

On the other hand, vast swathes of the population, including many Anatolian migrants to Istanbul, are traditionally Islamic in their outlook. Thus there are few strip clubs, brothels or adult venues in the city. The red-light district is in Aksaray, a western area of the Old City settled by East European immigrants. But illicit pleasure-seekers seek at their own risk – don't be surprised if that seedy hotel room you've just walked into comes with a hustler that is considerably more muscular and threatening than you bargained for.

NIGHTCLUBS

![360°] **360°** *(top)*
*Istiklal Caddesi Mısır Apartmanı,
7th & 8th floors, Beyoğlu
Tel: 00 90 212 251 1042
www.360istanbul.com
Open: daily, 7pm–3am*

The best nightclub in Beyoğlu, offering a touch of the glitz that you'd get at the Kuruçeşme nightclubs in a considerably cooler setting, is 360°, opened at the end of 2004. Set up by Englishman-turned-local Sashah Anton Khan, 360° occupies a spacious, totally modern, purpose-built floor above the lovely 19th-century Mısır Building on Istiklal Caddesi. As its name hints, the club's large terrace and glass walls allow an all-round panorama of the city, with especially nice views of the Golden Horn and the lovely belfry of next-door's St. Antoine Church. Inside, the design is coolly minimalist in foundation, with several more contemporary-cum-retro touches like the large, circular, sculptural light over the restaurant area. The restaurant offers an eclectic international menu featuring, among other things, sushi, steaks, Turkish dishes, and seafood. Just as extensive is the bar menu, which attempts to introduce several new cocktails to Istanbul as well as fruit frappés for the sensible non-drinkers out there, all of which are enjoyed by the generally very attractive crowd to the sounds of progressive house.

....

![Anjelique] **Anjelique** *(bottom)*
*Muallim Naci Caddesi,
Salhane Sokak 10, Ortaköy
Tel: 00 90 212 327 2844
www.istanbuldoors.com*

Open: daily, 7pm–4am

Mirrors are the leitmotif at Anjelique, ostensibly so that the club's terrific Bosphorus views are reflected and bounced around the place, but we all know it's so that neurotic Turkish TV stars can keep themselves calm throughout the evening with quick, unsubtle checks of their mascara or gelled-back hair (no gender prejudice here). Run by the Doors Group – which seems to be on a mission to stylise the social life of Istanbul's wealthy party crowd, and also own Vogue (see Eat) and A'jia (Sleep) – Anjelique is ultra-cool in its feel, the aforementioned mirrors set against white walls and touches of purple light. The restaurant on the terrace is typically full, but the bar and dance-floors are where the action is, and get going after midnight. Grooving alongside the slender models and beefy tanned male accompaniment are plenty of Istanbul's super-rich. On which note, if you're a guy and on the pull and you are not a) a Turkish celebrity, b) an A-list international celebrity (having been on an embarrassing reality TV show once doesn't count), c) playboy heir to a billion-dollar soap/ball-bearing/hemp manufacturing empire or d) combination of the above (extra points), then lie and pretend you are. If you are a lady with amorous intent, be warned that the kind of men you find at Anjelique are exclusively interested in tans, silicon and a minimal approach to clothing. This applies equally to Reina, Sapphire and Sortie.

....

Babylon *(top)*
Sehbender Sokak 3,
Asmalımescit, Beyoğlu
Tel: 00 90 212 292 7368
www.babylon.com.tr
Open: 9.30pm–2am Tues–Thurs,
10pm–3am Fri–Sat. Closed mid-July to
mid-September.

'Babylon turns Istanbul on' is the slogan, and while it's a little pat it's kind of true. Istanbul's premier live music venue attracts a great mix of acts from Scandinavian ambient outfits to African singer-songwriters: recent visitors include Manu Chao, IAMX and Kate Nash. Babylon is also famed for its club nights at which DJs belt out a similarly eclectic range of sounds: jazz, world music, electronica, drum 'n' base and house. Life mimics art in the diversity of the friendly crowd, stretching from groovy business types to hedonistic students – anyone who likes loud music and dancing, really. In drawing in punters from all over town to its industrial-like space, Babylon was instrumental (pun intended) to Asmalımescit's hyper-inflation-like rise to being party-central.

Ghetto *(left)*
Kamer Hatun Caddesi 10, Beyoğlu
Tel: 00 90 212 251 7501
www.ghettoist.com
Open: daily, 8pm–2am

Misnomer galore. Unless that is, the word "ghetto" conjures up images of a split-level interior, almost 150 square metres worth of dance floor, and a lofty, arching ceiling modelled after – you guessed it – Michelangelo's Sistine Chapel. The club, a former bakery, serves up world music, jazz, and Turk-ish rock. During the summer – theme alert – the action moves to the rooftop, where Ghetto's restaurant, Feraye, turns into a dance floor after 10pm. A new addition for 2010 was Metto. This traditional-style meyhane restaurant dishes up Ottoman and Balkan meze, perfect for nights of raucous singalongs to the fiddle and drum of Anatolian gipsy beats. In 2011 Ghetto's third-floor Session room chimed with a new appreciation of acoustic and one-off sets. Its retro stage and funky armchairs are the place to see experimental DJ sets, live concerts and other boutique events..

Indigo *(right)*
Akarsu Sokak 1-5, Beyoğlu
Tel: 00 90 212 244 8567
www.livingindigo.com
Open: 9pm-5am Fri–Sat. Weekday hours depend on concerts. Closed in summer.

Right off Istiklal Caddesi, Istanbul's premier venue for electronica also features live performances by local and foreign artists. If the martini-in-one-hand-cigarette-in-the-other-while-I-nod-my-head-style of dancing preferred by much of the Bosphorus crowd isn't what you're looking for, then Indigo is. Let your hair down, shove, be shoved, sweat, and enjoy. Music policy includes from Madness, Dexy's and Oasis so expect more bop than strop. Of late Indigo has been introducing more and more live acts from Turkish indie to modern Anatolian folk on its sizeable stage. Perhaps the club's most enduring attraction aside from the budget bottles of beer is the house pizza oven, which busts out slices of greasy margherita to those who've bopped their way right through dinner.

party...

133

Karga *(top)*

Kadife Sokak 16, Kadıköy
Tel: 00 90 216 449 1725
www.kargabar.org
Open: daily, noon–3am

Asia! Given all the hoopla about Istanbul being the only 'world city' straddling two different continents, its Asian shore remains largely ignored by most guidebooks, so don't be surprised if you can't find neighbourhoods like Kadıköy on so much as a tourist map of the city. According to lore, Kadıköy's original name – Chalcedon, or land of the blind – has to do with the fact that its first Byzantine inhabitants must have been blind to settle here, and not on the peninsula on the opposite European shore of the Bosphorus. These days, you'd have to be blind yourself not to give Asia a go, by day, by night, or indeed by both. Kadıköy might not yet be to the European side what Brooklyn has become to Manhattan, but – thanks to places like Karga – it's getting there. Unmarked, recognisable only by the drawing of a crow ('karga' in Turkish) hovering above its entrance, Karga is a Kadıköy institution, its walls thick with the drawings of avant-garde artists, its decks attended to by local DJs, and its stage home to grunge bands on the verge of a big break. Come here for lunch, stay for the film screening or art show upstairs, and top it all off with cheap drinks and a rowdy concert. If this isn't your cup of tea, plenty of other options are around the corner, with Kadife Sokak and the surrounding streets overflowing with pubs, clubs and restaurants. Unlike most of the nightspots on the European side, which draw in party-goers from all over the city and beyond, Karga and other Kadıköy joints serve a predominantly local clientele – a welcome respite from the see-and-be-seen crowd that often seems less focused on having a good time than on figuring out where to go next.

Nu Club *(bottom)*

Mesrutiyet Caddesi 67, Tepebasi
Tel: 00 90 212 245 6070
www.nupera.com.tr
Open: 11pm–4am Fri–Sat.
Closed June–November.

If it's not summer and you're in town of an evening searching for a little subterranean excitement, try Nu Club – small, loud and often densely packed with a smart, attractive clientele that generally ranges from late 20s to early 40s. The intimacy is all part of the attraction, especially on the dance-floor, which, though modestly proportioned, is usually lively. The DJs tend to put out a mixture of house and more dancey pop hits, and there's a strong Parisian connection thanks to some of the promoters, who regularly lure Gallic trendies over to take command of the music for a bit. In the summertime, the party moves upstairs, to the seventh-floor Nu Teras, complete with glass dance floor, two bars and fantastic views of the Golden Horn. Head chef Esra Muslu dishes out funky international cuisine at 67, the ground-floor restaurant.

NuBlu *(left)*
Jurnal Sokak 4,
Asmalımescit, Beyoğlu
Tel: 00 90 212 245 3800
www.nubluistanbul.net
Open: daily, noon–4am

Having recently found a new home next to Babylon – it was formerly located alongside the Bosporus clubs in Kuruçeşme – NuBlu is the lovechild of the well-regarded tenor saxophonist and producer Ilhan Ersahin, whose playing style, for the record, is influenced by John Coltrane and Joe Henderson. After the success of his first club NuBlu, set up in New York's East Village, where he also runs a record label, Ersahin thought he'd try his hand at the same thing at home.

Given the musical pedigree of its owner, it's no surprise that NuBlu plays a sophisticated mix of groove, reggae, pop and disco. The crowd is more bohemian and less flashy (not difficult) than the Bosphorus glitterati, but the music is better and the per capita botox consumption significantly lower.

....

Reina *(middle)*
Muallim Naci Caddesi 44,
Kuruçeşme
Tel: 00 90 212 259 59 19
www.reina.com.tr
Open: daily, 7pm–4am mid-May
to mid-Oct

Leila used to be king of Istanbul's nightclub hill but has now become Sor-

tie, lost some of its brand value and so surrendered the meritoriously glittering, fake tiara of victory to Reina. With its Bosphorus waterfront venue, its confusing array of expensive 'guest' restaurants and bars, and last, but certainly not least (and in fact first, in that it's plastered over the entrance), its enormous hoarding, Reina has all the necessary attributes of leadership. It's large, expensive and enormously popular with Istanbul's celeb-party crowd. The design is plush-minimal, complete with cream furniture and black stone decorative fireplaces that look as if they are from British Gas's Contemporary Range. But the décor isn't really the main attraction. For the etiquette of mating rituals in expensive Istanbul clubs, see Anjelique. Finally, as with Anjelique, if you have a yacht you can avoid the front-door heavies and glide into Reina's own docking bays (ring ahead to reserve your berth).

Sortie   *(right)*
Muallim Naci Caddesi 141, Kuruçeşme
Tel: 00 90 212 327 8585
www.sortie.com.tr
Open: daily, 6pm–5am

Until the mid-noughties Sortie was Leila, Turkish celebrity central and the most famous club alongside Reina on the Kuruçeşme strip. Now it's called Sortie and is Turkish celebrity central, only slightly less famous (for the moment). The patrons are happy to drop several hundred dollars a night each

137

on the overpriced food, Champagne and cocktails, but they – and you – are effectively paying for the company. Not the conversation, of course, which, even if it were worth listening to, is drowned out by the loud pop-pap broadcast by the DJs, but their aesthetic and social presence. Like its rivals, Sortie is certainly blessed by attractive customers and so worth a visit, along with all its rivals (just to make sure). Bring your Black AmEx, or just spray-paint your debit card.

Jon have played here, alongside some surprisingly good local acts. The crowd is your expected mix of students, rap neophytes – think eyebrows with shave lines, FUBU sweatshirts and Karl Kani jeans – and genuine aficionados.

Riddim *(left)*
Siraselviler Caddesi 35, Beyoğlu
Tel: 00 90 212 251 2723
www.riddim.com.tr
Open: 9.30pm–5am. Closed Mondays.

Riddim, a hop and a skip from Taksim Square, is indisputably Istanbul's go-to-spot for hip-hop, Turkish and otherwise. Ja Rule, Busta Rhymes and Lil

Zarifi *(middle)*
Çukurluçesme Sokak 13,
Çukurcuma
Tel: 00 90 212 293 5480
www.zarifi.com.tr
Open: noon–2am. Closed Sundays
and May–mid-Sept.

It's more of a restaurant than a club, but you should only book into Zarifi (rammed on prime nights, so booking is essential) if you're interested in a raucous night out involving a good bit of dancing and loud music, which is basically clubbing. The food – Turkish, Greek and Arabic – is perfectly good; though it's not a headliner on the bill,

it does come first. The very elegantly-decorated interior fills up around 9pm–10pm with a smart crowd, generally in its late 20s to 40s, with people typically dining in large groups. As the evening progresses and the meze are washed down with increasing amounts of rakı and wine, the in-house DJs crank up the volume on the Turkish and Oriental pop hits, and the fun starts. First, it's just a few more exuberant types waving their arms around to the music; then a few stand up; others get on chairs; and soon the tabletops are as crowded as the dance-floor. The peak comes when the live entertainment takes over from the DJs, especially when it's a band of attractive Roma drummers that beats out atavistic rhythms and send the place crazy. A good, totally unpretentious Turkish night out.

MUSIC CLUBS

Dogzstar   *(right)*
Kartal Sokak 3, 3rd floor,
Galatasaray
Tel: 00 90 212 244 9147
www.dogzstar.com
Open: depending on performance

A music club that prides itself on steering clear of mainstream music, Dogzstar hosts performers that run the whole gamut – from experimental jazz-playing art collective to Turkish ska group to Swiss indie band. Reggae and dub are perennial mainstays, however, and it's this rocksteady beat that drifts across the neighbouring alfresco bars and cafés most evenings. Tiny, crowded, noisy and fun, Dogzstar is tucked away on a cosy side street that's lined with cafés and restaurants and found off Istiklal. The shows are hit-and-miss, but the vibe is friendly and refreshingly

party…

139

unpretentious. Dress-down and leave the credit card at home.

 Jolly Joker Balans *(top)*
Balo Sokak 22, Beyoğlu
Tel: 00 90 212 249 0749
www.jollyjokerbalans.com
Open: 8pm–2.30am. Closed Mondays and Tuesdays.

Balo Sokak is party-central, slap-bang in the middle of barmy, boisterous Asmalımescit. But unlike many sweaty locales in this street, Jolly Joker takes its music policy a wee bit more seriously with a roster of Turkish groups and the odd international band with music ranging from rock and indie to fiery traditional folk. From Thursday to Sunday expect riotous – or tear-jerking if it's folk-time – ensembles with crashing guitars and soaring vocals cheered on by an up-for-it crowd. DJs fill in the gaps on other nights – when the atmosphere is, as ever, more student bop than poser's paradise.

 Nardis Jazz Club *(middle)*
Galata Kulesi Sokak 14, Galata
Tel: 00 90 212 244 6327
www.nardisjazz.com
Open: 7pm–1.30am. Closed Sundays.

At the top of one of the roads that slopes away from Galata Tower is the city's top jazz venue, Nardis Jazz Club, run by guitarist Onder Focan. The simple, contemporary fittings in the old building work well, but that's beside the point. This is a small but serious jazz club and not a place for chatting or admiring the décor. The music starts from 9.30pm onwards and is top-notch. You

can eat and drink (quietly), but book ahead if you want a table near the stage.

 Roxy *(bottom)*
Aslan Yatağı Sokak 3, Beyoğlu
Tel: 00 90 212 245 6539
www.roxy.com.tr
Open: 9pm–3am (5am Fri/Sat). Closed Sundays to Tuesdays and July–Sept.

In a side street off Sıraselviler Caddesi, Roxy is one Istanbul's best-known music and club venues, hosting bands, DJs and electronica outfits as well as more unusual theatrical performances. It's also a regular dance club playing an eclectic mix of funk, soul, disco, etc. that attracts a young, faithful following. And it's open until 5am on weekends if you're simply looking for that last, late-night round.

The return of the *nargile*,
by Kathryn Tomasetti

Up until the last decade of the 20th century, the tradition of smoking a *nargile* was a ritual appropriated exclusively by elderly Turkish men. *Nargile* cafés were synonymous with rampant, fruity clouds of tobacco smoke, each puff shrouding endless rounds of backgammon or glass after tiny glass of tea. To the rest of the country's population, the 'hubbly-bubbly' water pipe was considered utterly uncool: no hip *Istanbullu* – and certainly not one under the age of 60 – would be caught dead with a bendy length of pipe in hand. How times have changed.

The Turkish *nargile* – called a *hookah* or *shisha* in other Middle Eastern cultures – traces its origins back to India via Iran. The pipe is believed to have wafted its way across Asia Minor to the heart of the Ottoman Empire sometime during the early 17th century.

It was an immediate hit. The trend of smoking these ornate water pipes spread like wildfire across all social echelons of old Constantinople, with extensive and ostensibly strict rules established for the preparation and lighting the *nargile*. Tobacco had to be Iranian, sticky and moist; charcoal had to be oak. Sought-after artisans developed their own unique designs, handcrafting and carving individual elements for the pipes. So much so that owning a *nargile* – as well as when and with whom you smoked it – became the ultimate status symbol.

Turkophile and 19th-century French author Pierre Loti helped popularise the *nargile*. His regular haunt (see Pierre Loti Café) still remains one of the prettiest places in the city to puff away an afternoon. Diplomats, ex-pats and travellers were smitten too, and the trend spread to Paris, London and other European capitals at the start of the 20th century. However the advent of cigarettes, as well as the driving quest for modernisation during the Turkish Republic's early days, meant that by the 1940s these formerly beloved water pipes plummeted from the height of fashion to sadly passé. *Nargile* terrain beat a retreat into the tea gardens of male pensioners alone.

Seven decades on and trends have swung around yet again. Maybe it's because Turks are no longer looking west for inspiration, or perhaps it's a throwback to a (now) proud historical tradition. For many young Turks from more conservative families, it's definitely more acceptable to spend an afternoon puffing away rather than an evening supping *raki*. For whatever reason, *nargiles* are in style yet again. Smokers are on the up, with *nargile* cafés multiplying around town. Take your pick of old school or super cool – these days it's pretty much a given that while in Istanbul, you'll be keen to include at least a *nargile* experience or two.

No special skills are needed, but here's a quick prep to get you *au fait* with the water pipe's ins and outs. The *nargile* functions as tobacco (usually fruit-flavoured – apple, or *elma*, is the most popular) is loaded into the *lüle*, the bowl on the upper portion of the pipe. Burning charcoal is placed on top of the tobacco (in any café the charcoal is tended to courtesy of a special *nargile* waiter). The smoker inhales through a separate tube, pulling the smoke through the cooling water in the pipe's lower section, then into the tube for the eventual puff. Expect to spend around an hour smoking one complete *nargile*. The pipe is perfectly paired with a game or two of *tavla* (backgammon) – and every café has stacks of sets that you can borrow for free.

In Istanbul, Erenler Aile Çay Bahçesi is the place to go for a taste of times past. Near Sultanahmet's Grand Bazaar, it's one of the city's oldest *nargile* cafés. A large portion of the patrons here are locals, and it remains a good spot to take in the hard-core tradition of keeping a personal pipe at your favourite café.

Just west of the Istanbul Modern on the Tophane waterfront, a jumble of modern *nargile* bars, low-slung tables and rainbow-hued beanbags offer the fashionable smoker the most contemporary puffing experience. Hipster Istanbullus linger over their water pipes, gossiping or using the blanket WiFi to message, Facebook or check out videos online. The trendiest opt to smoke *nargiles* through fresh seasonal fruit like oranges or melon.

Nargile smoke may be smooth and cool, but we often find ourselves hankering to pair the experience with a cooling beer. As alcohol is frowned upon in traditional Islam (and even in moderate Turkey the drinking age was recently raised to a whopping 25 years old), the mix is definitely atypical. The raucous strip of bars that line the lower level of the Galata Bridge – although tending towards fluorescent, sometimes neon décor – is not only the most modern smoking spot in the city but also one of the few places that serve up both *nargiles* and bottles of Efes. This alcohol and tobacco combination, while hardly time-honoured, is a western import which may put a smile on some.

culture…

It has been Istanbul's fate, over centuries, to be at the epicentre of enormous shifts in geopolitical power from East to West and back again. The city was originally Hellenic, became subsumed and shaped by the Romans, who in turn were moulded by Eastern tradition before finally being supplanted by the Ottomans. After centuries of vitality, the late Ottomans crumbled before the ever-increasing Western powers while lapping up European ideas on art, architecture and high society at the same time. In the last major plot twist, coming after the Empire's disastrous defeat in World War I, Mustafa Kemal Atatürk, a gifted general, packed the last Sultan onto the Orient Express with a one-way outward-bound ticket and created the modern, Westernised republic that Turkey is today.

The good news for visitors is that the city still bears the mark of each culture that has lived within it, so that to walk through its older areas is to explore an open archaeological site in which the layers of history excite at every turn.

Aside from the awesome Hagia Sophia, much of old Byzantium lies hidden. The great Byzantine palace that once covered much of Sultanahmet is the city's greatest lost monument, although its substructures are still there, accessible through the odd cellar. For one of the most atmospheric – and touristy – trips back a millennia and a half, head down into the Basilica cisterns, which were lost for several centuries. At the Church of Christ in Chora, relatively neglected by visitors until recently, a stunning mosaic-lined interior breathes life into the Constantinople of antiquity.

The Ottomans took up the grand building tradition of the Romans with gusto, but it took them a century to match the challenge of the Hagia Sophia's dome and ethereal interior. Mimar Sinan, the great Ottoman architect, equal to any produced by Renaissance Europe, built the Süleymaniye Mosque for Süleyman the Magnificent. Sited on the city's highest hill, it is imposing, but as with the Hagia Sophia, it is the soaring lightness of its interior, an attempt to create a heavenly space on earth, wherein lies the genius of its architecture. In a new veneration of all things old – Ottomania is the popular expression – a wave of renovations have brought these buildings back to their best, the mighty Süleymaniye included.

Of the late Ottomans, the Bosphorus palaces, starting with the Dolmabahçe, are indicative of the era's last-gasp pomp. Eastern and Western architectural traditions are elegantly melded in Beyoğlu and along Istikal Caddesi, the European quarter's former Grande Rue de la Pera. Several Art Nouveau gems spread across Istanbul are reminders that early 20th-century Istanbul was as fashionable as any city in Europe.

In terms of contemporary Turkish life, Istanbul has evolved from a museum piece into a bastion of modernism over the last decade. The economy has boomed and Turks have once again been travelling abroad in huge numbers, importing fresh ideas at the same time. Patronage of the arts is a key concept for Istanbul's mega-rich and each major clan has supported its own popular museum. Backing the Pera Museum are members of the Koç family which is the power behind the Koç Group, Turkey's largest conglomerate, while its second largest, Sabancı Holdings, are benefactors to the excellent Sakıp Sabancı Museum. Still perhaps the top place to see contemporary Turkish art is at the Istanbul Modern (supported, of course, by another major family, the Eczacıbaşıs). Two new significant free art spaces opened in 2011, Arter and SALT, which have democratised the scene further still.

The Turkish art market is now worth an estimated $200-million and the London-based auction houses of Bonhams, Christie's and Sotheby's host yearly sales. The gallery scene, much of it spreading uphill from the Istanbul Modern, has grown to dizzying proportions, too. Interested parties should check out Galerist (Istiklal Caddesi 163, www.galerist.com.tr), Daire (Boğazkesen Caddesi 65, www.dairesan-at.com) and Galeri Artist (Ayazma Caddesi 4, www.galeriartist.com) for starters.

On the surface, Istanbul might not seem the most child-friendly of cities but Turks love little ones and they're welcome everywhere. The pint-sized sweep across Tur-key's greatest sights at MiniaTürk is the best child-specific destination, while the leafy Topkapı Palace grounds and the nearby Gülhane Park are perfect for a sprint around.

SIGHTSEEING

Approach to the city by water

Until the Orient Express pulled into Sirkeci Station in 1883 at the end of its maiden journey, most Westerners first saw Istanbul from the water. Today's taxi ride from Atatürk International Airport is more efficient but rather less spectacular. It is only by re-creating that approach to the city by sea – which at its simplest you can do by hopping aboard the ferry back to the Old City from the Asian shore – that you get a true hint of the psychological impact felt by generations of visitors on their first vision of the city. From the water, the massiveness of the Hagia Sophia, and the great Blue Mosque and Süleymaniye are all the more powerful and surreal, the city more exotic. Their effect on one admittedly famously romantic eye is recorded in Byron's epic poem Don Juan: 'The European with the Asian shore/ Sprinkled with palaces; the Ocean stream/ Here and there studded with a seventy-four;/ Sophia's cupola with golden gleam;/ The cypress groves; Olym-pus high and hoar;/ The twelve isles, and the more than I could dream...'

 Archaeology Museum *(left)*
(Arkeolojii Müzesi)
Yokuşu, Gülhane
Tel: 00 90 212 520 7742
Open: 9am–5pm. Closed Mondays.

It's unsurprising that a city with such a history should have such a superb archaeological museum. Nevertheless, its collection (of which only a fraction is on show) is world-beating with a breadth of exhibits to rival the Oriental sections of the British Museum, the Louvre or the Smithsonian. You could spend several days within its 20 galleries, but one of the highlights is its most famous artefact, the Alexander Sarcophagus. Part of the necropolis of the Phrygian Kings found in a Lebanese field just over a century ago, it is a 4th-century marble sarcophagus, its sides bearing exquisitely-carved bas-reliefs depicting Alexander the Great's wars with the Persians. Much to the chagrin

146

of its discoverers, though, it's not actually Alexander's tomb. After inspecting the museum's wonderful classical statuary, have a look at Istanbul through the Ages, a permanent exhibition that tells the story of the city through several evocative pieces, including a section of the great chain that the Byzantines used to pull across the Bosphorus to block invading ships. To end on a positive note, take a peek at the world's earliest peace treaty, the treaty of Kadesh agreed in 1269 BC between the Hittites and the Egyptian pharaoh Ramses II and carved into tablets on show in the next door building, the Museum of the Ancient Orient. The Tiled Kiosk alongside was built as an Ottoman-era party pad, but now houses an astoundingly beautiful collection of stained-glass, ceramic teapots and fine porcelain.

....

Atatürk Museum   *(right)*
Halaskargazi Caddesi 250, Şişli
Tel: 00 90 212 240 6319
Open: 9am–4pm.
Closed Sundays and Thursdays.

It's impossible to understand modern Turkey without understanding the remarkable Mustafa Kemal Atatürk. As a brilliant young general, he soundly defeated the Allies at Gallipoli and then rose up against the Greeks who occupied parts of Turkey after its defeat in World War I and booted them out. The last sultan soon followed them, with a one-way train ticket on the Orient Express. In 1923, Turkey became a secular republic and Mustafa Kemal adopted the name Atatürk 'Father of the Turks' and the presidency. Still more remarkable is that in seeking to reverse the decline of the late Ottoman period and in his attempt to build a modern secular industrial state, Atatürk re-forged an entire culture. He changed the language, exorcising the Arabic script, altered habits and costumes, and banned the word Constantinople and the seemingly innocuous fez among other things, and in doing so practically re-invented the Turkish identity. Atatürk's honorific title was well-deserved. He died in 1938, but Turkey is still enamoured with his image and memory. The museum is a short

culture

147

taxi ride away from Taksim Square and houses three floors of Atatürk memorabilia including, wonderfully, his underpants. While not the world's best museum, it's a good place to go to and think – and get to grips the legacy of the man.

The Bosphorus Tour *(top)*

The first words go to the 18th-century satirist and Istanbul diarist Lady Mary Wortley Montagu: 'The pleasure of going on a barge to Chelsea is not comparable to that of rowing upon the canal of the sea here, where, for twenty miles together down the Bosphorus, the most beautiful variety of prospects present themselves'. Indeed. Back then, the green and tree-lined shores of the Bosphorus – which stretches 14 miles from the Sea of Marmara to the Black Sea – were studded with villages and *yalıs*, the beautiful, wooden, sometimes fabulously ornate summer houses wealthy Ottomans built for themselves. On a sunny day, the Bosphorus is still as magical and there are plenty of wonderful sights along the way – the beautiful 19th-century Büyük Mecidiye Mosque by the first, massive suspension bridge in Oratköy, and the twin fortresses of Rumeli and Anadalou (edging the shores at the Bosphorus' second bridge and constructed by Mehmet the Conqueror in 1452 to knock out any ship daring to break his siege of Istanbul). Boats also steam alongside the decaying beauty of the Köprülü Yalı in Amcazade, the kitschy baroque Muhayyes Yalı in Yeniköy and Sultan Abdülaziz's summer palace in Beylerbeyi, as well as scooting past the major waterfront museums from Istanbul Modern to the Dolmabahçe Palace. Twice-daily tours leave from the Eminönü ferry terminal with a passenger pick-up in Beşiktaş. Private boat tours also depart from the same areas.

Church of Christ *(bottom)* in the Chora (Kariye Camii)
Kariye Camii Sohak 26, Edirnekapi
Tel: 00 90 212 631 9241
Open: 9am–7pm (until 5pm in winter). Closed Wednesdays.

Truly jewel-like, the modestly-sized Church of Christ in the Chora is a visual delight, adorned with what are possibly the finest remaining examples of Byzantine art in the world. The church's name is explained by a mosaic above the entrance that depicts the Virgin Mary shown with Christ in the womb. Inscribed are the words, 'container [chora] of the uncontainable'. The theme of the containers is taken up with gusto in mosaic scenes of miracles such as the turning of water into wine and the Feeding of the Five Thousand in which jugs of wine and baskets of bread take pride of place, all of which cast Tupperware in a new light. There is a mosaic depicting the Enrolment for Taxation, which one historian describes as possibly 'the greatest glorification of tax collection in the history of art'. The 14th-century art inadvertently owes its preservation to the Muslims who converted the place to a mosque, covering and thus protecting the frescoes and mosaics with plaster. Next door to this spellbinding museum is the Kariye Hotel, with its famed Ottoman restaurant Asitane. A few minutes away are Istanbul's ancient city walls.

culture...

Ancient City Walls

Stretching from the Sea of Marmara to the Golden Horn, these great city walls were built just in time by Emperor Theodosius II in the 5th-century to repel an attack by Attila the Hun. They formed the western boundary of the Old City for a thousand years until the Ottomans breached them with some finality in 1453. Today the ruins still give a sense of their once near-mythical indomitability. Better still, you can walk the length of the wall, sometimes on top of it, passing through some of the most diverse areas of the city, from the ex-Greek suburb of Fener through a predominately Kurdish neighbourhood, right down to the Yedikule Fortress by the Sea of Marmara. Notable points along the way include the Gate of Romanos, where Constantine XI, the last emperor, fell before Mehmet's army, and Edirnekapı, where Mehmet made his victorious entry after blasting the wall with a specially-made super-canon, Orban, which he had cast in Hungary. The gun was so large that it took three hours to reload but the damage is still in evidence today.

Dolmabahçe Palace   *(left)*
Dolmabahçe Caddesi, Beşiktaş
Tel: 00 90 212 236 9000
Open: 9am–4pm. Closed Thursdays.

The clearest proof of the Europeanisation of the Ottoman court came when Sultan Abdülmecit (1839–62) abandoned his ancestral home of the Topkapı – finding it a little too medi-

eval for his sophisticated Francophile tastes – and built the massive, baroque Italianate palace on the Bosphorus, nearer the modern action of Beyoğlu. It took 11 years to build and was finished just before the outbreak of the Crimean War, in time for Abdülmecit to receive the European emissaries of his allies in its vast throne room. The superbly self-important ornate, baroque and rococo style speaks of a building designed to impress through sheer visual attrition, hoping that the onlooker's quality-control mechanism will cease to function in the face of all those embellishments. Significantly for the palace's status in the national psyche, Atatürk died in a big walnut bed in a room on the second floor in 1938, today covered by a Turkish flag bedspread. Modern Turkey's founding

father also liked to dive into the Bosphorus and bob around in his rowboat from the palace's private jetty. Compulsorily guided tours in various languages depart from the main palace doors.

Galata Mevlevihanesi *(right)*
(Whirling Dervishes)
Galip Dede Caddesi 15, Tünel
Tel: 00 90 212 245 4141
Open: times vary

Whirling Dervishes! Along with everything else that smacked of the bad retrograde Ottoman days, the Whirling Dervishes were banned in the brave new world of the Turkish republic. Eventually, however, the government took pity on the hordes of visiting tourists and allowed the Galata Mevlevihanesi

– which reopened after extended renovations in July 2011 – to stage shows. Several other atmospheric venues now hold Dervish performances including Sirkeci railway station and, around the corner from the terminal, the Hodjapasha Culture Center, a 500-year-old Turkish bath. Founded by the Persian mystic Rumi in the 13th-century in Konya, eastern Turkey, the Dervishes are considered by some outsiders as an archaic bunch of hippies. They believe 'the fundamental condition of our existence is to revolve' and aim their revolutions towards attaining a trancelike communion with the powers on high. Wherever you find a performance, the spinning devotees make a breathlessly spectacular sight to behold.

Galata Tower *(top)*
Galata Square, Beyoğlu
Tel: 00 90 212 293 8180
Open: daily, 9am–8pm

Built in 1348 by the Genoese whose settlement lived in its shadow, the heavy cylindrical form of the Galata Tower was converted by the Ottomans into a prison for captives taken in battle. Nowadays, the leg-irons are gone but its Turkish management (possibly direct descendants of the original jailors) still inflicts punishment on foreigners in the form of a nightly theatrical 'touristic' entertainment, which includes harem shows and belly-dancing. However, if you visit during the day you can avoid its clutches and instead enjoy the fabulous 360-degree views, arguably some of the finest in the city. While you're up there, spare a thought for poor Hezarfen Ahmet Çelebi, who in 1630 slipped on a pair of homemade wings and swooped down over the city landing, it is claimed, in distant Üsküdar across the Bosphorus. New ideas were considered dangerous in the Ottoman court, however, and Sultan Murad IV had Çelebi exiled and the theory of flight banished for several centuries.

Hagia Sophia *(bottom)*
(Ayasofya Müzesi)
Sultanahmet
Tel: 00 90 212 528 4500
Open: 9am–6pm. Closed Mondays.

If you have time to see just one building in Istanbul, head to the Hagia Sophia. For a thousand years, it was the largest building on earth, although the Hagia Sophia's power didn't derive from gross size alone. The Byzantine historian Procopius witnessed this miracle rising from the ground: 'A spherical-shaped domed standing upon this circle is exceedingly beautiful; from the lightness of the building, it does not appear to rest on a solid foundation, but to cover the place beneath as though it were suspended from heaven by the fabled golden chain'. Built by the great Byzantine emperor Justinian (it was finished in AD 537), it's hard to overestimate its importance over the subsequent centuries in the imaginations of both friends and foes of Constantinople, generating the kind of awe in contemporaries that New York's skyline would for those who have never seen a city before. But the real magic, as Procopious understood, was inside. The idea of the interior was to be a place of awe that in its spaciousness, the improbability of its dome, the gleam of its gold mosaics

culture…

in the candlelight, and the scent of incense, transported, almost literally, the worshipper to a heavenly place. Such responses belong to another time, but the architecture and the decoration – particularly the Empress Zoe and Comnenus mosaics – are still otherworldly.

Hippodrome (left)
At Meydanı, Sultanahmet

All that is left of Constantinople's once mighty Hippodrome, which by the 4th-century could seat 100,000 spectators, is the long, rectangular area of At Meydanı (Horse Square) in front of the Sultanahmet Mosque. It was the *spina*, or central reservation, around which the charioteers would race with reckless ferocity, and on which the spoils of war would be heaped up for all to see. The vertical relics that survive are among the most ancient artefacts in the city, including the 5th-century BC Serpentine Column, nicked from the Temple of Apollo at Delphi, and the Egyptian obelisk, carved around 1,500 BC and filched from Karnak. The emperor Theodosius had it set on a marble pedestal carved with scenes celebrating his enjoyment of the races. The noise and excitement inspired by the Romans' favourite pastime was channelled into an intense rivalry between the two chariot-racing factions, the Blues and the Greens, which dominated Byzantine life. The Niké Riots, which briefly threatened the throne of Justinian, ended in the massacre of 35,000 of the Green faction by the triumphant Blues, which puts even the rivalry between Istanbul's big football teams – Galatasaray, Fenerbahçe and Beşiktaş – into perspective.

Kız Kulesi (The Maiden's Tower)
Üsküdar
Tel: 00 90 212 342 4747
www.kizkulesi.com.tr

One of Istanbul's most famous landmarks is Kız Kulesi, the Maiden's Tower, but better known in the English-speaking world as Leander's Tower. The latter name refers to the old Greek legend of Leander who died swimming to see his beautiful lover, Hero. It's familiar to many visitors as the watery prison that M is incarcerated in at the end of the Bond film, The World is Not Enough. In any case, the building – bobbing in the Bosphorus just offshore of Üsküdar – is actually a small, squat tower, built during the last century, which has done nothing more heroic than serve as a lighthouse. Nevertheless, it's a nice place to sip tea and contemplate the views. Shuttle boats leave every hour from the ferry terminals of Kabataş in European Istanbul and Salacak on the Asian shore.

Milion *(right)*
near Divan Yolu, Sultanahmet

At the crossroads opposite the Hagia Sophia, walking towards Diyvan Yolu, there is an unassuming broken stone column rising up from a bricked recess. It is the Milion or milestone, once probably tiled in gold. In AD 324 Constantine made it the point from which all distances in the Roman Empire would be measured.

MiniaTürk
İmrahor Caddesi, Sütlüce
Tel: 00 90 212 222 2882
www.miniaturk.com.tr
Open: daily, 10am–7pm (8pm Sat–Sun)

Bored with worthy monuments? Pushed for time? Then MiniaTürk, located on the Golden Horn, could be the ticket for you. This large park contains 105 splendid models of the historical and cultural sites of Turkey all at

culture

1:25 scale. See the Aspendos Theatre, the Süleymaniye Mosque, the Sumela Monastery, as well as a mini Bosphorus complete with sailing ships. There is also a miniature railway network, a motorway with moving vehicles and an airport with thousands of human figures and planes. While it's aimed predominantly at children, it's fun for grown-ups, too, not least because of the summer-only go-kart track out front. The Rahmi M Koç Museum (www.rmk-museum.org.tr) nearby is also fun for kids, with airplanes, a model railway track and a real-life submarine to explore.

on the European shore of the Bosphorus in the summer of 1452 signalled the doom of Byzantium. Built in only four months to face Anadolu Hisarı across the narrowest point of the Bosphorus, it was part of Mehmet the Conquerer's plan to isolate Constantinople by destroying any ship attempting to ferry supplies into the city. Thus it was nicknamed Bogazkesen (the throat-cutter) and immediately on completion sunk a foolhardy Venetian merchant ship with its long-range cannon. Now it plays host to more pacific activities, such as open-air theatrical and musical events through the summer nights.

 Rumeli Hisarı
Yahya Kemal Caddesi,
Rumeli Hisarı
Open: 9am–4.30pm. Closed Wednesdays.

The appearance of the massive form of Rumeli Hisarı (Hisarı meaning castle)

 Şakirin Mosque   *(left)*
Karacaahmet Cemetery,
between Üsküdar and Kadıköy
Tel: 00 90 212 521 1121
Open: no formal visiting hours but
avoid Friday morning prayers.

This visually spectacular mosque is the city's most groundbreaking religious building in more than a century for a variety of reasons. Set in the leafy tranquillity of the Karacaahemet cemetery, the mosque's glass walls – each one lacquered with a Koranic verse – are bounded only by the trees beyond. Inside the finely engraved minbar prayer pulpit looks like an installation from a contemporary art gallery, while looping chandeliers hang lopsided from a spellbinding dome that topped off the complex in 2009. Perhaps more interesting is the fact that its western-educated designer, Zeynep Fadıllıoğlu, wanted to design a mosque, adding to a design portfolio that includes many of the city's coolest stores, hotels and restaurants. More surprising still is the fact that Zeynep is a woman, and the Şakirin is Istanbul's first female-designed mosque. Subsequent coverage of this rather radical model has been overwhelmingly positive, and dozens of young architects have submitted their own avant-garde designs to the city's religious authorities.

....

St. Stephen's Cathedral (right)

Mürsel Paşa Caddesi 85-7, Fener
Tel: 00 90 212 521 1121
Open: no formal visiting hours.

The cathedral of St. Stephen of the Bulgars on the shore of the Golden Horn is notable on two counts. It is one of the few examples of neo-Gothic architecture, but more impressive is the fact that it's a pre-fab, constructed entirely out of cast-iron sections, cast in Vienna and floated to Istanbul down the Danube on a hundred barges. It was built – or, rather, bolted together – in 1871 for the Bulgarian community who were allowed by the Ottomans to split from the Greek Ortho-

Church. Despite being neo-Gothic and made of iron it's a pretty church still used by the dwindling local Bulgarian community and busloads of pasty pilgrims from across the Bulgarian frontier.

Süleymaniye Mosque *(middle)*
Tiryaki Çarşısı, Süleymaniye
Tel: 00 90 212 514 0139
Open: daily, 9am–7pm but avoid
Friday morning prayers.

The crowning achievement of starchitect Mimar Sinan, the Süleymaniye is the Ottoman riposte to the Byzantine showpiece of the Hagia Sophia. Unlike early Christian builders, Sinan was interested in making an impact externally, locating the mosque on the Old City's highest hill and designing a series of smaller domes cascading off the central structure and supporting its weight. But like the Hagia Sophia, whose footprint it roughly follows, it is the interior that really matters. Its sense of the space and the elegant lightness with which the vast span and size of the dome is supported are an amazing architectural and engineering feat, an expression of power and technological sophistication at once subtle and awesome. The scene is all the more vivid following a thorough four-year renovation, which was completed in late 2010. More than any other individual in its history, Sinan has left his physical mark on the city as author of a vast number of buildings (477 throughout Turkey) and is the enduring symbol of the glory of the reign of Süleyman the Magnificent. Born of Christian parents in 1490, he was taken into imperial service as a child, working as a military engineer before becoming Ottoman

Chief Architect in 1538. He designed up until his 99th birthday, and is buried in a simple tomb near Süleyman himself in the expansive Süleymaniye grounds.

Blue (Sultanahmet) *(top)*
Mosque
At Meydanı, Sultanahmet
Tel: 00 90 212 518 1319
Open: daily, 9am–9pm (7pm Nov–Apr)
but avoid Friday morning prayers.

Built by Mehmet Aga (a pupil of Sinan's) for Sultan Ahmet I and completed in 1616, the Sultanahment Mosque quickly became known as the Blue Mosque, owing to the profusion of blue Iznik tiles that cover much of its interior. The six minarets with which Mehmet Aga furnished the mosque were a cause of controversy, as the Grand Mosque at Mecca, the holiest site in Islam, also had six at the time. A tad too assuming on Ahmet I's part, perhaps, but he was possibly the most pious of sultans and even attempted to ban alcohol within the Empire – never a popular move. However, the Blue Mosque's interior lacks the elegance, gracefulness and engineering genius of either the Hagia Sophia or the Süleymaniye. The dome here is far more obviously supported by the thick pillars, thus spoiling the conceit of a sacred, inhumanly wrought architecture. It is still pretty impressive from the outside, though, and Sultan Ahmet's legacy lives on in the district's assumed name: Sultanahmet.

Topkapı Palace *(bottom)*
Museum
Sultanahmet, Eminönü

159

Tel: 00 90 212 512 0408
www.topkapisarayi.gov.tr
Open: 9am–7pm (Harem until
4pm). Closed Tuesdays.

Built by Mehmet the Conqueror and embellished by countless other sultans, the Topkapı Palace was the epicentre of the Empire for some 400 years. Sited on a promontory overlooking the confluence of the Golden Horn and the Bosphorus, the Topkapı owes its form more to a military encampment than to the grand sacred or monumental architecture of the Greeks or Romans. It's best described as a collection of ro-coco mansions and bling-tastic kiosks, where everything from meetings of state to palace intrigues and circumcision ceremonies would have taken place. Aside from the treasure room, the armoury and the sultans' dress room (a bevy of pajama-chic costumes if ever there was), one wing to look out for is the palace kitchen, which reopened afresh in 2011. It reportedly contains the worlds' greatest collection of Chinese porcelain outside of Asia, much of it dating from the time when the Ottomans were convinced that the china's blue celadon glaze would discolour at the first contact with poison. The Topkapı is vast and often packed with visitors, so to maximise your viewing pleasure try going as early or as late as possible. If you have limited time, have a quick stroll around the complex and then dive into the famous Harem (you need an additional ticket for this area). This complex of 300 intensely-decorated rooms is joyously decadent. It's easy to imagine its steamy confines awash with the beautiful women gathered from the Christian borderlands of Armenia, Ukraine and Hungary, especially in the secluded outdoor pool to the rear where the young maidens would frolic in the nude under the sole eyes of the sultan and his team of eunuch retainers.

 Turkish and *(left)*
Islamic Art Museum

At Meydam 46, Sultanahmet
Tel: 00 90 212 518 1805
Open: 9am–5pm. Closed Mondays.

The gloriousness of this museum's building didn't do any favours for its first owner, Ibrahim Pasa, Grand Vezir to Süleyman I. The Sultan was convinced by his scheming wife Roxelana to get rid of Ibrahim whose vaunting ambition, she felt, was symbolised by the grandeur of his home. The deed was done via ritual strangulation, a common theme in medieval Ottoman high society. Now this old palace overlooking the Hippodrome houses a collection of assorted examples of Islamic arts: manuscripts, carpets, miniatures, woodwork, metalwork and glasswork, which originated from all corners of the Empire. Especially notable are old, large and glorious Seljuk and Ottoman mosque carpets.

 Underground Cistern   *(right)*
(Yerebatan Cistern)

Yerebatan Caddesi, Sultanahmet
Tel: 00 90 212 522 1259
www.yerebatan.com
Open: daily, 9am–6.30pm

These subterranean cisterns date from early Byzantine times but were only rediscovered in the 16th-century by visiting Frenchman Petrus Gyllius. The explorer had little time for the 'Carelessness and Contempt of everything that is curious in the inhabitants [of Istanbul]' and went poking around in cellars instead. He found this 6th-century part of the Byzantine's complex, an impressive cistern system that housed the city's reservoirs of water, together with a few odd-looking fish whose descendants still swim between the columns today. Most visitors will already be familiar with the cavernous column-strewn passages as they feature in the Bond film From Russia With Love as MI6 agent Kerim Bey's escape route from the Soviet Embassy. Queues for the cisterns snake around the block at peak times, but their eeriness and sense of discovery makes it well worth the visit.

ART

Arter
Istiklal Caddesi 211, Beyoğlu
Tel: 00 90 212 243 3767
www.arter.org.tr
Open: 11am–7pm (8pm Fri/Sat).
Closed Mondays.

The latest and greatest in a rash of contemporary art spaces that litter the buzzing Beyoğlu area. And like many other of the area's galleries, Arter pulls in the curious with accessible exhibitions, free entry, late opening hours and a central location. Laid out over four floors inside a big bougeois mansion, the centre is a supreme space, especially for the themed group exhibitions that are the specialty of the house. German mastermind René Block curated the opening show, which was cheekily named Starter, and recent displays have been curated with the help of such luminaries at Madrid's Thyssen-Bornemisza Museum. Like many art institutions in Istanbul, Arter is patronised by the truly wealthy, in this case the Koç family, which has been offering classic and contemporary art before the public's gaze since the 1980s.

İstanbul Modern
Meclis-I Mebusan Caddesi, Liman İşletmeleri Sahası Antrepo 4, Karaköy
Tel: 00 90 212 334 7300
www.istanbulmodern.org
Open: 10am–6pm (8pm Thurs).
Closed Mondays.

Visual art has been the most internationally successful of Turkey's contemporary art forms. Such artists as Kutlug Ataman, Taner Ceylan and fashion-designer-turned-artist Hussein Challayan are big names on the global gallery circuit, while the domestic scene has taken root on the streets leading up from the Istanbul Modern. Indeed, the museum's opening in late 2004 – built by the philanthropic Eczacıbaşı family, the country's foremost cultural patrons – has shone a spotlight on the scene and incubated dozens of bright young artists. On permanent exhibition is New Works, New Horizons, a vivid passage of 19th- and 20th-century Turkish art. The older paintings smack of foreign ideals, as young artists returned from Paris and Vienna importing figurative styles and pastoral panoramas with them. Temporary exhibitions in the former warehouse's basement are bold, playful and strong on photography and video. A cinema, a Bosphorus-side bar and a cracking restaurant complete the mix.

Pera Museum
Meşrutiyet Caddesi 65
Tepebaşı, Beyoğlu
Tel: 00 90 212 334 9900
www.peramuzesi.org.tr
Open: noon–7pm (6pm Sun).
Closed Mondays.

Housed in a mansion row near the Pera Palace Hotel (which includes the Istanbul Culinary Institute and the Italian Cultural Centre), the Pera Museum brings classic and contemporary art to the masses. The first two floors are based around solid permanent exhibitions, including Portraits from the Empire, a pictorial history of Istanbul that illustrates how the city's splendour grew from rococo wooden palaces within the city walls to meaty mansions up and down the Bosphorus. The exhibition's most famous piece, The Tortoise Trainer, lies incongruous as a portrait as opposed to a landscape canvas. This endearing painting is the work of Osman Hamdi Bey, who set up Istanbul's Archeological Museum to house relics pulled in from across the Empire as the Ottoman era slowly collapsed at the end of the 19th-century. The top two floors are dedicated to temporary shows with a timeless twist – nothing too edgy here. Recent exhibitions have taken in the work of Frida Kahlo, Diego Rivera, Fernando Botero, Marc Chagall and the engravings of Pablo Picasso. The museum's ability to haul in such wonderful works is in no doubt thanks to the patronage of the Suna and İnan Kıraç Foundation. Suna Kıraç is ranked as one of Turkey's wealthiest individuals and is an ardent philanthropist as well as chairwoman of the Koç Group, the country's largest conglomerate.

SALT

İstiklal Caddesi 115, Beyoğlu
Tel: 00 90 212 292 7605
www.saltonline.org
Open: noon–8pm Tues–Fri;
10.30am–6pm Sat

Freshly unveiled in April 2011, SALT Beyoğlu is Istanbul's newest contemporary gallery, funded by prominent Turkish bank Garanti. SALT – not a reference to the seasoning but a translation of the Turkish word for 'pure' – is sprinkled over six floors of the 19th-century Siniossoglou Apartmanı building. Three levels of exhibition space

are sandwiched between the innovative Walk-In Cinema, complete with art house documentaries and plush velvet benches, and a nascent 'experimental edible' rooftop garden. SALT's opening show by late Turkish artist Hüseyin Bahri Alptekin was stellar; expect similarly cutting-edge exhibitions in the future. SALT Galata (Bankalar Caddesi) opened in October 2011. This second gallery space also holds the Ottoman Bank Museum, an auditorium, research facility, library and an awesome rooftop restaurant purveyed with perfection by the Istanbul Doors group (of Vogue and Zuma fame). Exhibitions are held over both beautiful spaces.

Sakıp Sabancı Museum

Sakıp Sabancı Caddesi 42, Emirgan
Tel: 00 90 212 277 2200
muze.sabanciuniv.edu
Open: 10am–6pm (8pm Weds).
Closed Mondays.

This all-encompassing contemporary art museum started life as a summer mansion of the Khedive clan, the Istanbul-based hereditary rulers of Egypt which left several royal piles along Bosphorus. It also served as the Montenegrin Embassy before being purchased in all its vastness by Hacı Ömer Sabancı, a leading industrialist and the initial force behind the Sabancı Holdings Conglomerate. From 1966 the next head of the family, Sakıp Sabancı, called it home and filled it with his expansive collection of Turkish art and calligraphy. A public museum since 2002, the permanent collection also includes works by Raphael and local

163

boy Osman Hamdi Bey, plus photographic and archaeological exhibits. The museum has the space to display serious temporary shows including major Dalí, Rodin and Picasso exhibitions. A day of culture can be complemented by lunch in the museum's acclaimed MüzedeChanga restaurant, tea in the winter garden or a show in the Seed, an architecturally-advanced art and meeting space that opened in 2011.

CLASSICAL MUSIC

 Atatürk Cultural Centre
Taksim Square, Taksim
Tel: 00 90 212 251 5600
www.iksv.org

On Taksim Square, the brutalist 1970s form of the Atatürk Cultural Centre – known locally as the AKM – is the city's premier performing arts venue. It's also home to the State Opera and Ballet, the Symphony Orchestra and the State Theatre Company and is the place to come to see performing arts. An extensive refit that began in 2008 wasn't ready in time for the city's 2010 Capital of Culture celebrations, but was completed for the 12th Istanbul Biennial in late 2011.

Süreyya Opera House
Bahariye Caddesi, Kadıköy
Tel: 00 90 212 346 1531
www.sureyyaoperasi.org

This grand old Opera house and sometime movie theatre took over the baton from the AKM when the latter shut up shop for refurbishments in 2008. A full calendar of Italian and German opera, ballet and theatre is performed within the pompous interior just off Kadıköy's main thoroughfare.

TRADITIONAL MUSIC CLUBS

 Adali Meyhane
Refik Saydam
Caddesi 153, Tepebaşı
Tel: 00 90 212 243 1126
www.adalimeyhanesi.com

Around the corner from the Pera Palace is Adali, where you might like to sample Turkish folk music with a beer or two. The packed program includes a Friday-night fasıl show, Saturday evening *buzuki* performances and regular folk nights throughout the week. Typically for such places, it also serves up some good, simple Turkish dishes like bean stew, grilled fish, *şiş* kebab and aubergine salad, all laced with a generous dose of rakı.

 Kallavi
Aytar Caddesi 3,
Levent İş Hanı, Levent
Tel: 00 90 212 251 1010
www.kallavi.com.tr
Open: noon–3pm, 7pm–1am.
Closed Sundays.

Why simply have a cultural experience when you can have a gastronomic, cultural and entertainment experience all in one? After a trip to one of the many

meyhanes that play Turkish folk or its related musical cousin *fasıl* – which combines strains of classical, gypsy and folk
– it's not hard to see why Western-style
pop hasn't come to dominate Turkey's
music culture completely. Kallavi, a
meyhane, in the ritzy suburb of Levant a
few Metro stops north of Taksim, is one
of the best places to go to hear *fasıl*. As
your meal progresses and increasing
amounts of rakı are consumed, the *fasıl*
band trots out and skilfully starts building up the tempo until the little reserve
that the Turks possess is completely
swept away, along with the tables, in
an orgy of handclapping and jigging
about. Reservations recommended.

shop…

Shopping is in the lifeblood of Istanbul. Much of the city's historical fame and fortune is owed to its perfect position, poised at the centre of ancient trade routes between East and West. Even now the Bosphorus presents a constant parade of container ships ferrying everything from agricultural produce to iPods, to and from the Black Sea ports and the world at large.

The city has always consumed its fair share of that trade, and all the exchange had to be housed somewhere. So with considerable foresight Mehmet the Conqueror founded the Kapalı Çaraşı – the Grand Bazaar – in 1461. It is now the oldest shopping mall in the world, a city unto itself of around 5,000 shops, attracting tourists and locals alike with the rarefied allure of fine carpets, precious antiques and artfully wrought jewellery, as well as the quotidian promise of acres of fake label handbags and knock-off designer clothes. Finding one's way through the bewildering array of stores and products, the noise, the hawkers and the essential haggling requires a tough sensibility, but a visit to what is the greatest Oriental bazaar of them all is rightly considered de rigueur.

Other bazaars in the old city also deserve attention. The Arasta Bazaar, originally built to help finance the next-door Blue Mosque, is a small but high-quality and genteel alternative to the Kapalı Çarşı (salespeople are banned from harassing passersby). It houses some of the city's most reputable dealers in carpets, rare Turkish and Asian textiles and ceramics. Among the heady mix of sweets and spices on sale at the Egyptian Spice Bazaar, near Galata Bridge, are superb honeys, sun-dried chilli peppers, nuts, coffee and other earthy products. The relative cheapness of the caviar, both Iranian and Russian (from the Caspian), deserves special mention and perhaps the preparatory packing of cool bags.

Over the bridge, Beyoğlu offers more contemporary attractions. Towards the top of the steep hill that climbs from Galata Tower into town is a cluster of music shops, including those selling specialised Turkish instruments. Nearby quality antiques and

high-class (some quite pricey) retro items, reminders of Istanbul's cosmopolitan 19th-century past, fill the charming shops and boutiques of Çukurcuma, a once dilapidated area recently gentrified into an Istanbullu equivalent of Portobello. Meanwhile the huge, pedestrianised thoroughfare that is İstiklal Caddesi promises everything one could want (and much more one does not want) from a modern high-street shopping experience. Be sure not to miss Hacı Bekir, the eponymous confectionary founded in 1777 by the inventor of *lokum* (Turkish Delight), amid the confusion of shop fronts.

Fashionistas and label addicts will have to head still further north where the chic district of Nisantası is home to sleek, international and home-grown designer boutiques as well as upmarket department stores such as Beyman. The highlights here are those vendors who creatively update their Turkish and Ottoman heritage, including designer Gönül Paksoy, whose contemporary-fashioned Ottoman fabrics would look equally good framed as worn, and her sister Sema Paksoy, who incorporates exquisite historical fragments into her contemporary jewellery works. Alternatively, cross the Bosphorus to Bağdat Caddesi, a tree-lined boulevard edged by designer boutiques. A cornucopia of shops, cafes and restaurants, it's rarely visited by foreign tourists.

SULTANAHMET

■ Arasta Bazaar *(top)*

Built to help finance the Blue Mosque's charitable projects, the Arasta Bazaar (www.arastabazaar.com) is a single alleyway of shops running alongside the mosque's eastern wall. It houses some of the most respected merchants in Istanbul and also has the delightful advantage of having banned touting among its tenants. If you're pressed for time and can't do the Grand Bazaar properly (or can't face it) then this petite shopping experience is a good, quick alternative.

Galeri Cengiz (155-157) – run by business partners, both called Cengiz, who are among the most respected carpet dealers in the city.
Iznik Classics (67 & 73) – high-quality, hand-painted ceramics, as well as reproductions of antique Iznik tiles.
Jennifer's Hamam (43 & 135) – traditional hamam towels, hand-woven in cotton, linen, bamboo and silk, as well as laurel and rose oil soaps, scrubbing mitts and luxury robes.

■ Egyptian Bazaar (Mısır Çarşısı)

Also known as the Spice Bazaar, the Egyptian Bazaar is an L-shaped hall located by the New Mosque, near Galata Bridge in Eminönü. It's always packed with tourists (blame yourself – we do) and superficially appears to be full of the rubbish that tourists love to buy. However, there are some excellent food shops and delis, which should not be missed. If you get hungry looking at all that food, you can head upstairs to the famous, still smart and attractive Pandeli restaurant. Alternatively, find and study the wares of one of the leech sellers to be found among the pet merchants. That might put you off eating for a while.

Cankurtaran Gida (33) – exquisite honey from all over Turkey.
Erzincanlar (2) – superb deli for honeycomb and hard Turkish cheese.
Hayat (8) – make like Bernie Ecclestone and pick up your utterly indulgent caviar here; also purveyors of fabulous Turkish Delight (honey, raisin, pistachios…).
Malata Pazarı (40-44) – for dried fruits and nuts, including delicious apricots, figs stuffed with hazelnuts and almonds.
Papagan Kuruyemiş (65) – nuts, mulberries, figs and other delights.

Off the Egyptian Bazaar

Kral (Hasırcılar Caddesi 6) – family-run spice shop selling top-quality saffron, spicy red pepper, hand-picked mint and local teas.
Kurukahveci Mehmet Efendi (Tahmis Sokak 66) – tiny shop selling the city's finest Turkish coffee since 1871.

■ Grand Bazaar *(bottom)* (Kapalı Çarşı)

The spiritual home of shopping in Istanbul, the Grand Bazaar is an extraordinary city unto itself, divided into mini-suburbs of one trade or another. At its heart is İç Bedesten (Inner Bazaar),

shop...

the ancient and comparatively genteel home of many of the market's most respected merchants. It's here you'll find many of the bazaar's highest value items, antiques, metalwork and curios. To its north and west are the carpet dealers, to its south and east, jewellers and gold and silver merchants. Textile and leather dealers are found primarily in the alleys at the market's extreme west. Shopping in the Grand Bazaar seriously takes at least half a day, allowing time for looking, comparing, getting tired, looking again, haggling, arguing, and possibly storming off and starting the whole process somewhere else. But that would be bad manners, as you shouldn't enter into protracted bargaining unless you intend to buy. For that vital rest, bite to eat and stimulating coffee, look for the Fes Café (Halıcılar Caddesi 62 just north of İç Bedesten), Julia's Kitchen (Keseciler Caddesi, south of İç Bedesten) or Sark Kahvesi (Yağlıkçılar Caddesi 134, on the corner of Fesciler Caddesi). With around 5,000 shops (including 1,600 jewellers alone) on 60 streets, the selection below amounts only to a few highlights.

Abdulla Natural Ürünler (Halıcılar Caddesi 58-60) – 100% natural, handmade textiles and soaps.
Adıyaman Pazarı (Yağlıkçılar Caddesi 74-46) – top dealer in Gaziantep weaves, the highly-coloured, traditional, Ottoman textiles.
Barocco Gümüş (Kalcılar Han 31) – master silversmith Baruyr Ortainceyan's shop; simple, affordable pieces alongside the fabulous, ornate and expensive.
Dervis (Keseciler Caddesi 33–35) – excellent quality textiles, including

cotton towels from Bursa, as well as natural soaps.
EthniCon (Takkeciler Sokak 58–60) – contemporary and highly fashionable patchwork kilims; fixed prices.
Galeri Şirvan Halıcılık (Halıcılar Caddesi 50-54) – respected carpet dealer.
Kalendar Carpets (Takkeciler Sokak 24-26, www.kalendercarpet.com) – top (and therefore pricey) Anatolian carpets; located on main carpet alley.
Kurtoğlu Halı (Zenneciler Sokak 24) – well-designed carpets and kilims.
Lumes (Zincirli Han 16) – dazzling Ottoman-style chandeliers.
Pako (Kalpakçılar Caddesi 87) – beautiful handbags and purses.
Sisko Osman (Zincirli Han 15) – eponymous shop of the Bazaar's most famous carpet dealer; highest quality.
Yörük Deri (Kürkçüler Çarısı 17) – specialist in ethnic rugs, especially from the Caucausus.

BEYOĞLU

İstiklal Caddesi

Beyoğlu's great pedestrianised artery, İstiklal Caddesi, is a vast and very long, glaring parade of storefronts, neon signs and people. It's also the shopping centre of choice for most Istanbullus. For offbeat labels and homegrown designers, head to the back streets that surround the Galata Tower, just a couple of minutes south of İstiklal Caddesi.

Atlas Pasajı (131) – covered arcade crowded with alternative clothing stalls, vintage finds and jewellery, tucked be-

Cukurcuma

ÇUKUR CUMA
CADDESİ

Y-LONDON

shop...

Nisantasi

hind the entrance to Atlas Sinema.

Emgen Optik (65) – fashionable sunglasses in case you left yours at home.

Hacı Bekir (83) – Hacı Bekir, chief confectioner for the Ottoman sultans, was the inventor of *lokum* (Turkish Delight); the business, started in 1777, is still in the family and the produce should banish any lingering bad memories caused by trying Fry's Turkish Delight (a horrible British chocolate bar with a sickly, gooey centre purportedly inspired by Turkish Delight) as a child.

Mahmut Kundura (35) – quality, bespoke gentleman's shoes.

Mango Outlet (81) – deeply discounted women's clothing from Mango's previous season, on sale in the store's basement.

Mavi Jeans (215/A) – top trendy Turkish denim brand, big in the US and comparatively inexpensive here.

Oxxo (146) – pretty, inexpensive clothing aimed at younger women.

Robinson Crusoe (195/A) – excellent English-language bookstore, with plenty on Istanbul and Turkish history, plus a superb fiction selection.

Terkoz Çıkmazı – an alley running off İstiklal near glassware shop Pasabahçe (nr. 150), where you get high-street fashion factory seconds for next to nothing.

Off İstiklal Caddesi

Butik Katia (Danışman Geçidi 4/C, Galatasaray) – purveyors of the most famous hats in town and family-run since the 1940s; bespoke and ready-to-wear for fashionable women.

Homer Kitabevi (Yeni Çarşı Caddesi 12/A, Galatasaray) – excellent English-language bookshop with particularly

good academic and current affairs sections; the place to go for books on the politics of Turkey and the Middle-East.

Ottomania (Sofyalı Sokak 30-32, Asmalımescit) – valuable antiquarian Ottoman items; essential for serious collectors.

Ümit Ünal Butik (Ensiz Sokaka 1/B, Tünel) – unusual mens- and womenswear from one of the city's top young designers.

Galata

Atelier 55 (Serdar-i Ekrem Sokak 55) – both Turkish and international-designed clothes, accessories, ceramics and homeware.

Laundromat (Galip Dede Caddesi 93/b) – funky clothing and accessories store, with particular emphasis on felt, silk and paper creations.

Paristexas (Camekan Sokak 4) – shoes, totes and women's clothing from international big names, plus more obscure Japanese labels, tucked into a tiny boutique behind the Galata Tower.

Simay Bülbül (Serdar-ı Ekrem Sokak, on the corner of Şah Kulu Bostan Sokak) – brand-new spot showcasing elegant eveningwear and soft leather bags.

ÇUKURCUMA

Down the steep hill from the Galatasaray Lycée is Çukurcuma, a once slum-like antiques district that has gone through a dramatic rise in fashionability and property prices thanks to the influx of trendy creatives. The area is now equivalent to London's Notting Hill, except in Çukurcuma the antiques and bric-à-brac are more authentic and still relatively affordable. Not for long, though...

▌ Faik Paşa Yokuşu

One of the best roads for browsing and purchasing, though there are great shops scattered throughout Çukurcuma's winding streets.

A La Turca (4) – showroom (and owner's house) full of decorative objects (don't miss the stacks of antique ceramics in the basement).
Accenturc (6) – sculpture, lighting, furniture, painting and jewellery all on show.
Hakan Ezer (5) – furniture and interior designer, well known for his traditional yet sophisticated PERA collection.
Hall (6/1) – Ottoman and contemporary homeware, collected and sold by New Zealand-born interior designer Christopher Hall.

Elsewhere in Çukurcuma

Leyla (Altıpatlar Sokak 6) – range of handmade clothes and fantastic hats.
Selden Emre Antik Shop (Cami Sokak 13) – reputable and quality antiques and curios dealer.
Stoa Design (Hayriye Caddesi 16/A) – sculptural furniture from designer/sculptor Tardu Kuman.

NIŞANTAŞı AND TEŞVIKIYE

Fashionistas and visitors for whom the bazaars of the Old City sound like a panic-inducing nightmare should head straight for the smart residential and commercial districts of Nişantaşı and Teşvikiye, where Istanbul's haute bourgeoisie roam freely..

■ Abdi İpekçi Caddesi

Abdi İpekçi Street is the closest the city has to Bond Street or Madison Avenue, though it's a good dealer smaller, leafier and nicer. This avenue is where Turkey's top designers show off their stuff alongside the usual list of well-known international brands.

Beymen (23) – newest and classiest branch of top Turkish department store.
Cengiz Abazoğlu (20/A) – wild women's eveningwear from the eponymous haute couture designer.
Hakan Yildirim (23/3) – up-and-coming fashion guru, creating very high-end womenswear.

Elsewhere in Nişantaşı and Teşvikiye

Arzu Kaprol (Atiye Sokak 9) – top Turkish fashion designer with international following.
Derin Design (Şair Nedim Caddesi 20/D) – custom-made sofas that can be delivered to anywhere in Europe within six weeks.
Ela Cindoruk & Nazan Pak (Atiye Sokak 14/B) – small and trendy jewellery boutique.
Gönül Paksoy (Atıye Sokak 6/A) – unique fashion designs based on contemporary reinterpretations of Ottoman clothes.

shop...

Sema Paksoy (Atıye Sokak 9) – modern jewellery designer incorporating ancient symbols and motifs.

SODA Istanbul (Şakayık Sokak 37/1) – boutique selling a range of creative jewellery from various local designers

Zeki Triko (Akkavak Sokak 63/E) – premier and stylish Turkish swimwear label.

BAĞDAT CADDESI

South of Kadıköy and Moda on Istanbul's Asian shores, Bağdat Caddesi is leafy, lined with lovely high-end boutiques and definitively off the tourist radar.

Raşit Bağzıbağlı (35/2) – sleek and sexy women's clothing, with haute couture creations available by appointment only.

Triko Mısırlı (404/A) – purveyor of classy knitwear since 1951.

Vakko (422) – huge name in Turkish fashion, selling a range of mens- and womenswear, leather, perfumes, silk scarves and other accessories.

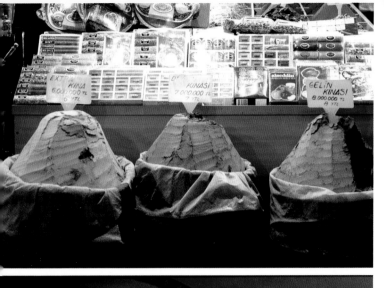

Grand Bazaar

play...

There is only one major exception to the Turks' general disregard for sport, be it active participation or passive appreciation – football. Istanbul's three famous teams, Beşiktaş and Galatasaray from the European side, and Fenerbahçe from the Asian, are feared both on and off the pitch. An Istanbul derby, if you can catch one during the season, which runs from August till May, is a sight (and sound) to behold. The Beşiktaş stadium near the Dolmabahçe is the most accessible.

Apart from the odd kid trying to maim passing tourists with a football, you are unlikely to see much sporting action on the Istanbul streets. Joggers are regarded as dangerously eccentric and gyms are only a recent addition. There are some pool tables, however (try the bars on Istiklal Caddesi), and backgammon sure does exercise those fingers. But with the recent increase of major sporting events in Istanbul from the Formula 1 race to the basketball World Championship, sporting options are bound to become more extensive over time.

More joy is to be had on the therapeutic front. Swimming provides a pleasing break from the hustle of the big city. The absolutely stunning pool at the Çırağan Palace or the ultra-chic pool on Su Ada, the pontoon-cum-island that floats just offshore from the stretch of night clubs in Kuruçeşme, are the best options. The nearest sandy beaches and their adjacent hip beach clubs lie along the Black Sea coast at Kilyos. Most locals cool off on the Princes' Islands, a 30-minute boat ride away from the Kabataş or Yenikapı ferry terminals.

Then there is, of course, the *hamam*, or Turkish bath, experience, which involves lying around on heated marble slabs in a large and beautiful stone room, and, if you wish, being soaped and massaged. Once, all Turks visited the baths and a century ago there were several thousand in Istanbul, but advances in mass-market plumbing put paid to the *hamam* as a truly popular destination. Now only about a hundred locales are still going strong, and the best known among them survive on tourist trade, meaning they are relatively expensive and can provide poor service.

Pick the wrong *hamam* and you will find yourself going through the tired motions of an ancient ritual – being ripped off. In some, the charade of a wash 'n' rub is almost entirely dispensed with; in others, the 'masseurs' tread a fine line between massage and physical assault. However, Cağaloğlu and Galatasaray *hamams* are showcases of the aesthetic beauty and atmospheric power of the old *hamams* and the levels of service should be acceptable, if expensive.

To guarantee more therapeutic results, however, the inauthentic but gentler and more careful *hamam* experiences offered by hotels such as Edition, Four Seasons and the Çırağan are recommended. Meanwhile, spas – those arrivistes of the luxury hygiene scene – have arrived all across Istanbul, but when in Rome…

BASKETBALL

Though a firm second to football, basketball is popular in Turkey. The three big Istanbul football teams have their own basketball teams, as do Efes, the beer manufacturer. The season runs from October to June.

BEACHES

Istanbul is surrounded by water and has more shores than one could hit in a month. The Black Sea beach clubs at Kilyos – in particular, buzzing Solar Beach (www.kilyossolarbeach.com) – are your best bet for a romp in the sand. But if you just want a cooling dip, your best bet is the Princes' Islands, an archipelago of four big and five tiny islands bobbing in Sea of Marmara. Boats take around 45 minutes from the Kabataş ferry terminal, stopping in quiet Kınalıada, leafy Burgazada, shabby-chic Heybeliada and bustling Büyükada. All have cute little towns offering tasty fish lunches, plus beach clubs that can be reached either by free shuttle boat or by horse-drawn carriage (cars being banned on all of the islands).

FAST CARS

Turkey welcomed its first Formula 1 Grand Prix race in 2005 at the newly-built Istanbul Park Circuit (www.istanbulparkcircuit.com), a 45-minute drive from Kadiköy. Races take place in early May and the circuit is a challenging one.

FOOTBALL

Football is the Turkish sport, in the sense that the Turks don't really play any others (except for basketball). Still, at least they're good at it. Turkey surprised the world, but not themselves, by coming third in the 2002 World Cup, but has stumbled in the international arena in the last decade. At home domestic rivalry between Istanbul's three main teams is famously fierce. Galatasaray is traditionally the club of the city's upper-crust, thanks to the club's historic connection with the elite Galata Lycée. Fortunately for visiting fans, it moved out of the feared Ali Sami Yen stadium into the slightly less daunting Türk Telekom Arena in 2011. Fenerbahçe, on the Asian side, is traditionally the army's team and has long been the strongest club in Turkey. Beş iktaş meanwhile, are the cool kids on the block, yet perennially place third. The football season runs from August to May.

Beşiktaş

Inönü Stadium, Dolmabahçe
Caddesi, Beşiktaş
Tel: 00 90 212 310 1000
www.bjk.com.tr

The 'Black Eagles' of Beşiktaş are the Chelsea of Turkish football with a wealthy support base, a downtown stadium and a history of punching below their weight in the domestic Süper Lig and Turkish Cup. Atatürk's former club have put in a good few seasons of late however, pipping the mighty Galatasaray up the road as European Istanbul's premier squad and tripping up mighty Manchester United in the 2009 Champions League.

A small intimate stadium lets fans get within touching distance of the players.

Fenerbahçe

Sükrü Saraçoglu Stadium, Kadiköy
Tel: 00 90 216 330 8997
www.fenerbahce.org

The grand dame of Turkey's Süper Lig had their Juventus moment in 2011 as sordid details of match fixing and league rigging boosted Turkey's usually slack summer newspaper sales. But Asian Istanbul's super squad have lorded over all and sundry from their ritzy Kadıköy base for over a century and are still country's most successful club by some margin – possibly as their garish fluorescent yellow kit causes glare-induced headaches in opposing teams.

Galatasaray

Türk Telekom Arena, Aslantepe
Tel: 00 90 212 688 0223
www.galatasaray.org

The 'Lions' of Istanbul have been reduced to pussycat status in recent years but once cast a shadow of Turkey – and Europe – as Istanbul's most feared club, not least because of their cauldron-like fortress of a stadium, the Ali Sami Yen. Nicknamed 'Hell' by its supporters, the pressure cooker atmosphere has contributed to notable victories over Barcelona, Real Madrid and Manchester United. The great Hakan Sükür – who ran for a seat in Turkey's parliament in 2011 – gave much of his gifted career to the club and is still awarded semi-divine status.

GOLF, HORSERIDING AND TENNIS

Kemer Golf and Country

Tel: 00 90 212 239 7010
www.kg-cc.com

Established in 1995, the swanky Kemer Golf and Country Club is the city's premier country club (without, admittedly, facing too much competition for the title) and the best place to go if you fancy a round on the green. Located north of the city towards the Belgrad Forest, which borders the Black Sea, it has an 18-hole course, the largest number of tennis courts in Turkey and an equestrian centre. The Club is currently expanding its remit to take in horseback riding, wellness and sailing, so watch this space.

GYMS

Most hotels have great workout spaces, with the more expensive options boasting cutting-edge gym facilities. Gyms are otherwise rare in Istanbul but these options are tip-top.

Marmara Istanbul

Taksim Square
Tel: 00 90 212 334 8300
www.themarmarahotels.com

One of best gyms in town has the full panoply of modern gadgetry and equipment, professional instructors, a good view over Istanbul and nice aquatic options like a sauna, Jacuzzi and outdoor pool. Day passes cost 40TL.

play...

179

Mars Athletic Club

Kanyon, Buyukdere Caddesi, Levent
Tel: 00 90 212 353 0999
www.marsathletic.com

The city's newest, coolest gym is in its ritziest shopping mall, Kanyon, allowing shoppers to duck into a Pilates class before lunch at Le Pain Quotidien. It also offers yoga, a sun terrace and a lap pool. One of five branches in town. Day passes cost 100TL.

HAMAMS

Early on, the Turks perfected the old Roman institution of the steam bath, encouraged by the Islamic belief that physical cleanliness is close to godliness, as well by the enjoyment of a good old soak. Like the classic Roman bath, a proper *hamam* has three rooms: the hot room (caldarium) for getting all steamed-up and subsequently massaged; the warm room (tepidarium) for washing; and the cool room (frigidarium) where one could relax a bit before changing and heading to the *camekan* (reception-cum-lounge area). Traditionally, the experience didn't stop there, for until the infernal 20th-century brought modern plumbing to Turkey, the *hamam* was a major social hub, where you would hang out with your friends (same sex, of course – men and women were segregated either in unisex baths or using the same baths at different times) and talk over tea.

Numbering more than 2,500 a century ago, today there are only around a hundred working *hamams* left in Istanbul. Most in the central areas, and certainly those in the Old City, survive almost exclusively on the custom of tourists who are after an authentic Turkish experience. Sadly, all that easy tourist money has corrupted many *hamams*, turning them into rip-off joints with (ironically) poor hygiene and lazy masseurs. Others survive in more working-class districts where the baths still have a community function. Don't expect any fashionable and/or wealthy Turks you know to be impressed by your foray into local culture when you tell them about visiting a *hamam*. With little regard for political correctness, they regard *hamams* as the preserve of the undesirables (the poor, gays, etc.) and tourists.

Despite all this negativity, it's worth visiting a *hamam* at least once, especially those baths that are architecturally stunning. For all their faults, the more touristy ones are at least easy to use.

Expect to pay around 40TL for entrance, with another 20TL for a 15-minute massage. Each *hamam* has a menu of service options, but in practice that essentially means a choice between DIY or hiring a masseur. Don't be afraid of insisting on better service if you feel it appropriate. Alternatively, for the hygiene equivalent of Russian roulette, try going to a non-touristy *hamam* where the menus are only in Turkish and then order at random. Will you get a pedicure or an all-over-body depilation? It's all part of the fun.

Büyük Hamam

Potinclier Sokak 22, Kasımpaşa, Beyoğlu
Tel: 00 90 212 238 9800

The imaginatively-titled 'Big Hamam'

is one to try if you want a non-touristy *hamam* that is relatively central. Built by Sinan, it might be big but it's still pretty.

Cağaloğlu Hamam

Prof Kazım Gürkan Caddesi 34,
Cağaloğlu, Sultanhamet
Tel: 00 90 212 522 2424
www.cagalogluhamami.com.tr

Built in 1741 by Sultan Mahmut I, and untouched since then, the Cağ aloğlu Hamam is the city's most famous and one of its most attractive. Ten minutes up the road from the Hagia Sophia, it's brought in tourists for centuries, including, apparently, Tony Curtis, famous for his enjoyment of baths. Though the service can be mediocre, this is a great *hamam* to try.

An alternative to the old purpose-built *hamams* is to visit the mini-*hamams* run by many of the top hotels as part of their fitness centres. Service is completely personal but more expensive. Try the *hamams* at the Çırağan Palace and Swissôtel.

No *hamams* are officially gay-only, and the managements wouldn't admit it, but the following are well known and popular in the gay community:

Tarihi Çeşme Hamamı

Yeni Çeşme Sokak 9, Karaköy
Tel: 00 90 212 252 3441

Discreet male-only *hamam* in the warren-like streets of lower Karaköy. This traditional steam bath pulls in an older – and normally rounder and

hairier – clientele who will be suitably aroused by younger foreign visitors. As welcoming and steamy as Beyo ğlu's volley of more outré *hamams*.

Aquarius Sauna

Sadri Alisik Sokak 29, Beyoğlu
Tel: 0212 251 8924
www.aquariussauna.com

Anything goes Turkish bath with suitably homoerotic Greco-Roman statuary, plus private cubicles with mini-Ottoman loungers. Small pool, large Jacuzzi, weights room and sauna, all of which get charged with male testosterone on a nightly basis. Massage and services available on request.

RUNNING

Jogging was once considered a bizarre activity in Turkey, undertaken only by foreigners, children and the criminally insane. Istanbul running club Adım Adım (www.adimadim. org) seeks to change attitudes with regular group runs through town and in the gorgeous Belgrade Forest. Istanbul's October marathon (www.istanbulmarathon.org) is the only event of its kind to cross two continents, as tens of thousands of competitors stream across the Bosphorus Bridge.

SKI

Skiing down Uludağ near Bursa, an hour's ferry ride from Istanbul then a cable car up to 2,000-metres, is loads of fun, with old-school ski lifts and cosy little hotels (www.

uludaghotels.com). It's also popular with Middle-Eastern residents, who can travel visa-free to Turkey for their first sight of snow.

SPAS

Spas are generally the refrain of Istanbul's top hotels, which can offer hamams, swimming pools and great après-spa facilities in with the package.

Çırağan Palace Spa
Çırağan Caddesi 32, Beşiktaş
Tel: 00 90 212 326 4646
www.kempinski.com/istanbul

The plush five-star Çırağan Palace boasts outdoor massage, a heated infinity pool and *hamams* fit for a sultan (or, indeed, a sultana).

Edition Espa
Büyükdere Caddesi 136, Levent
Tel: 00 90 212 317 7700
www.editionhotels.com

This superspa spreads five floors underground and has leather floors and horsehair walls to soak up any negative ions floating around. Aside from the Espa treatments and lounging rooms, there's a snow room and a water jet pond.

Four Seasons Spa
Çırağan Caddesi 28, Beşiktaş
Tel: 00 90 212 381 4000
www.fourseasons.com/bosphorus/spa

The spa complex at the Four Seasons Bosphorus is a temple of calm. Treatments include O2 Awakening and Cit-

rus Peel, but it's the three *hamams*, the chillout booths – with great magazines and mini reading lights – and massive pool that rank it among the city's best.

SWIMMING

Swimming is about the easiest sporting or pseudo-sporting activity you can do in Istanbul. All the large hotels (Edition, Hilton, Pera Palace, etc.) have pools of one sort or another. These, however, are the best:

Su Ada
Kuruçeşme
Tel: 00 90 212 263 7300
www.suadaclub.com.tr

Su Ada (it translates as 'water island') is a swish open-air swimming and general loafing joint housed on a pontoon floating in the Bosphorus. Although thoroughly modern, a swimming pool has been moored up here in some shape or form for nearly a century. Complimentary boats shuttle visitors across from the Kuruçeşme shore. Rates are around 70TL per day, or 90TL at weekends.

Çırağan Palace
Çırağan Caddesi 32, Beşiktaş
Tel: 00 90 212 326 4646
www.kempinski.com/istanbul

The Çırağan Palace's 33m pool is a spectacular place for a swim, bordering the Bosphorus and separated from it by the thinnest of margins. It is costly, though, at around 100TL for a day pass, although it means you can also use the Jacuzzis, steam rooms and indoor pool

play...

info…

CRIME
Istanbul is a relatively safe city, especially given its size. Some outlying neighbourhoods are slightly rougher than the centre. Obviously, do not wave your money around in touristy areas.

EMERGENCY NUMBERS
Police:155, Fire:110, Ambulance:112

FERRIES AND BOAT TRIPS
The main ferry docks on the European shore are Eminönü (Sultanahmet side) and Karaköy (Beyoğlu side). From these spots, ferry boats operated by İstanbul Deniz Otobüsleri (www.ido.com.tr) will take you to Üsküdar, Haydarpaşa train station or Kadiköy (running from north to south) on the Asian shore and over to the Princes' Islands. Ferries offering a Bosphorus cruise to the mouth of the Black Sea leave from Eminönü several times a day, starting at 10.30am. The full cruise, up and back again, takes six hours (just go south to north if pushed for time and take a taxi back).

MONEY
The Turkish lira (TL) has stabilised over the last decade and wild currency fluctuations are, hopefully, a thing of the past. At the time of writing (autumn 2011) the Turkish lira was worth: £1 = 2.5TL, US$1 = 1.6TL, €1 = 2.25TL

PRONUNCIATION
Key to making yourself understood when attempting Turkish words and names is knowing how to pronounce the language. All Turkish words are spelt phonetically, so it is relatively straightforward. Special Turkish characters, however, are pronounced in the following fashion:

c – 'j' in 'jerry'
ç – 'ch' as in 'cheese'
ğ – silent but elongates the proceeding vowel; so 'Beyoğlu' is pronounced 'Bey-o-loo'
ş – 'sh' and in 'shed'
ö – like the German 'oe' in 'Goethe'
ü – 'oo' – an elongated sound – as in 'boo'

TAXIS

Taxis are plentiful, relatively cheap and metered. Most taxi drivers are perfectly hon-
est but especially in touristy areas you should make sure that the meter (taksimetre)
is being used. If drivers try to haggle or set a price, insist they use the meter; don't
be soft if you feel you've been ripped off – take down the driver's name and report
them swiftly to the police. The rate is 2.5TL minimum and a one-way journey from
the Blue Mosque to Beyoğlu should cost around 15TL. Atatürk International Airport
is 25-kilometres from Sultanahmet and the journey should cost around 50TL. It
takes 30-45 minutes, depending on traffic. Beware the rare taxi driver trick where
the driver swaps your 50TL note with a 5TL one – then requests additional pay-
ment. The two notes look similar so count them out clearly when paying to avoid
any confusion.

TELEPHONE

To phone Istanbul from abroad dial 00 + 90 (country code) + your number. For the
international operator dial 115.

TIPPING

Tipping of 10% is standard and expected in cafés and restaurants, but not necessary
in bars or taxis.

TRAMS AND METRO

The Metro system is coming on leaps and bounds. Of most use to visitors is the
Tram that buzzes from the Kabataş ferry terminal by the Dolmabahçe Palace past
the Karaköy fish market, the Galata Bridge, the Topkapı Palace and Hagia Sophia,
the Grand Bazaar and historic Istanbul. The fastest Metro line currently links Şişhane
station in Beyoğlu with Taksim Square, Nişantaşı and the shopping malls of Levant.
It will loop across the Golden Horn en route to the airport by 2013. Another Metro
line currently under construction along the depths of the Bosphorus will link Europe
and Asia by rail for the first time in history, again in 2013.

WiFi

Most of Istanbul is wired up and almost every hotel, restaurant and bar offers free
WiFi, known simply as 'wireless' in Turkish. The Beyoğlu area basks under a municipal WiFi cloud and there are plenty of calm cafés should you need to make a Skype
call or blast off an hour of work.

notes…

index...

187

Hedonism /hedoniz'm/

'The philosophy that pleasure is the highest
good and proper aim of human life.'
– Oxford English Dictionary

Hg2 Corporate

Branded Gifts....

Looking for a corporate gift with real value? Want to reinforce your company's presence at a conference or event? We can provide you with branded guides so recipients will explore their chosen city with your company's logo right under their nose.

Branding can go from a small logo discreetly embossed on to our standard cover, to a fully custom jacket in your company's colours and in a material of your choice. We can also include a letter from your CEO/Chairman/President and add or remove as much or as little other content as you require. We can create a smaller, 'best of' guide, branded with your company's livery in a format of your choice. Custom guides can also be researched and created from scratch to any destination not yet on our list.

For more information, please contact Tremayne at tremayne@hg2.com

Content licensing....

We can also populate your own website or other materials with our in-depth content, superb imagery and insider knowledge.

For more information, please contact Tremayne at tremayne@hg2.com

Hg2|Cape To...   Hg2|Par...   Hg2|London   Hg2|Marra...   Hg2|Milan

Hg-Who?

Welcome to the world of Hg2 – the UK's leading luxury city guide series. Launched in 2004 as the *A Hedonist's guide to...* series, we are pleased to announce a new look to our guides, now called simply Hg2. In response to customer feedback, the new Hg2 is 25% lighter, even more luxurious to look at or touch, and flexible, for greater portability. However, fear not, our content is still as meticulously researched and well-illustrated as ever and the spirit of hedonism still infuses our work. Our brand of hedonism taps into the spirit of 'Whatever Works for You' – from chic boutique hotels to well-kept-secret restaurants, to the very best cup of coffee in town. We do not mindlessly seek out the most expensive; instead, we search high and low for the very best each city has to offer.

So take Hg2 as your companion to a city. Written by well-regarded journalists and constantly updated online at www.Hg2.com (register this guide to get one year of free access), it will help you Sleep, Eat, Drink, Shop, Party and Play like a sophisticated local.

"Hg2 is about foreign life as art" **Vanity Fair**
"The new travel must-haves" **Daily Telegraph**
"Insight into what's really going on" **Tatler**
"A minor bible" **New York Times**
"Excellent guides for stylish travellers" **Harper's Bazaar**
"Discerning travellers, rejoice!" **Condé Nast Traveller**